THE BOOK OF
STRESS
SURVIVAL

THE BOOK OF
STRESS
SURVIVAL
How to Relax and Live Positively

Alix Kirsta

Foreword by Michael van Straten
Photography by Fausto Dorelli

GUILD PUBLISHING LONDON

A GAIA ORIGINAL

From an original idea by Lucy Lidell

Photography by Fausto Dorelli

Editorial: Phil Wilkinson

Design: Kate Poole

Illustrations: Eugene Fleury
                Andrew MacDonald
                Joe Robinson

Direction: Joss Pearson
                David Pearson

This edition published 1987 by
Book Club Associates
by arrangement with Gaia Books Ltd.,
and Allen & Unwin Ltd.

Printed in Great Britain by
Purnell Book Production Limited
Member of the BPCC Group

About this book

The Book of Stress Survival is divided into four sections. The first is called *How Stressed Are You?* It describes the causes of stress and uses questionnaires to help you pinpoint the areas of your life that are particularly stressful and lead you to the chapters of the book that will be most helpful. The second section, *Stress-proofing Your Lifestyle*, shows the many preventive measures you can take to minimize the stress in your life. All the major areas of lifestyle are covered, from personal relationships, work, and time management, to the alterations you can make to stress-proof your home and the steps you can take to eliminate stress-inducing foods from your diet. The third section, *Ways to Relax*, illustrates a generous selection of relaxation techniques, including both simple and more strenuous exercises, meditation, and yoga. You will be able to use this section to choose the techniques that suit you best to do regularly, and you will also find techniques that you can use occasionally to help you calm down when life gets fraught. The final section of the book, *High-stress Situations*, is the place to turn for succinct advice on a variety of stress-related problems from illnesses, panic attacks, and depression, to stresses at work and in the environment.

Note on the exercises   If you have any injury or chronic illness, consult your physician before attempting the exercises in this book.

Foreword

"The ultimate measure of a man is not where he stands in moments of comfort and convenience, but where he stands at times of challenge and controversy" Martin Luther King

At moments of comfort and convenience stress is not a problem, but when challenge and controversy stare us in the face, the way in which we react, physically, emotionally, and spiritually, is the measure of our success in dealing with stress. Stress is a part of everyday life, and our bodies' responses to stressful stimuli have always played a key role in mankind's survival.

The "Fight or Flight" response which prepares our bodies for instant reaction at times of danger, and which our bodies produce without conscious effort or command, is the root cause of all the problems associated with our growing inability to cope with the stresses produced in industrialized western civilization. This remarkable ability to react instantly to challenge becomes counterproductive when it is impossible to choose either "Fight" or "Flight", when the only option is to "grin and bear it" or "grit our teeth" and "soldier on"–all expressions which betray the emotions. Many people are ill-equipped to deal with excessive stresses, and stress-induced illness is growing to epidemic proportions. Heart attack, high blood pressure, insomnia, PMT, menopausal problems, sexual disorders, skin compaints, digestive and bowel disturbances, asthma, migraine, and arthritis can all be directly linked to, or caused by, poor coping with stress.

The idea that these stress-related disasters are the exclusive province of the high-powered executive is just not true. No one is immune to this plague, and it is found on the factory floor, in the typing pool, at the kitchen sink, in the elderly and in the young, as well as in the boardroom.

Whilst attitudes to the overstressed patient are thankfully beginning to change, the orthodox medical approach frequently fails to recognize or deal with the root of the problem. The symptoms are treated but not the patient. The physician may not recognize the effects that the patient's mental state are having on his or her body, whilst the psychiatrist may well ignore physical disease and concentrate on the patient's mental problems. The epidemic of stress disorders is only equalled by the pandemic of prescriptions for antidepressant and tranquillizing drugs and the consequent dependence on these by millions of people.

Sweeping the dirt of stress under the pharmacological carpet with behaviour-modifying drugs is not the solution for the vast majority of people. There is no better example of the need for a holistic approach to health than in this field of stress disorders. There is no single answer to dealing with the vast range of problems stress produces, but the most important steps that any of us take along the road to coping with stress are to recognize it, to understand it, to use "good" stress to our advantage, to deal with "bad" stress, to cope with stress in our family, work, social and environmental situations and, above all, to help ourselves.

Alix Kirsta has provided us with a means of achieving this. From acupressure to meditation, diet to massage, through loving and working, her book is a comprehensive guide to understanding, living with, and coping with stress. Time is a pressure in any busy practice, and I know that this practical information will help my patients immeasurably. This book should be in every home, and on every health professional's bookshelf to remind us all that we are not the only ones who suffer stress at work.

Michael A. v. Stratton.

Contents

Introduction

Stress has been with us since the beginning of time.
Part of our response to any challenge or stimulus, it has
proved a positive force, aiding our continued survival
and providing a dynamic that distinguishes between the
active "business" of living and mere passive existence.
Shaping our lifestyle, setting the tempo, and determining
the rhythm at which we live, stress can generate the
impetus necessary to convert thought into action,
whether that action is making love, conducting an
orchestra, running a race, escaping from fire or flood,
or meeting a deadline.

But today life's challenges are far more complex than
they used to be, while life itself is altogether a harsher,
less natural process than it used to be. Living in an age
of immense and increasingly rapid change, we are subjected to greater, more insistent and inescapable
pressures to adapt, keep up, and compete—in short to
survive—than at any other time. Achieving the right
balance between too much and too little stress has
become an integral challenge of life in the 1980s. This
is a particular problem for people who find themselves
living a highly pressurized life—performers, journalists,
sportspeople, surgeons, and top-level managers and
directors. They usually find that the benefits of this
type of existence are inseparable from its drawbacks.
In fact some stress researchers suspect that many of us
are becoming addicted to our own increased levels of
stress hormones, depending on constant challenge as a
self-prescribed antidote to the intolerable prospect of
boredom.

The cost of stress

The human cost is severe. In America, the estimated
annual cost to industry of combined absence from
work, health charges, increased insurance, and
diminished productivity, is thought to run close to $75
billion. The cost of stress-related coronary heart
disease alone is about $30 billion. In Britain, at least 40
million working days are lost each year due to the
effects of stress, and it is estimated that stress-related
illness costs the medical and social services an average
of £55 million per year, accounting for a loss of 2-3 per
cent in the gross national product. The term "stress

burnout" is clearly no longer a meaningless cliché. It has become an established medical entity.

But stress is not only a problem for people living in the fast track. Those who suffer excessive monotony, boredom, or frustration because of insufficient stimulus or challenge also become ill frequently. This can be through lack of arousal or as a result of the anger or anxiety they feel at having little control over how they live and work. The boredom, envy, and loss of self-esteem that result from unemployment are also common sources of stress today.

So for most of us it is difficult to find the perfect balance between too much challenge and too little. Coping is made all the more difficult because we are often unconscious of the stress we are suffering. We have become adept at sublimating the effects of stress through motives such as ambition, perfectionism, and dedication to work. Yet the effects of "masked stress" are all the more pervasive for being hard to identify.

Answers to the stress problem

What is the solution? The thing that is common to all sufferers from stress–whether the over-stress of the fast track or the under-stress of boredom and frustration–is a feeling of not being in control of your life. If you think of the people you know who can handle significant amounts of stress and avoid its damaging effects, they are usually men and women who maintain a strong sense of commitment to their work and other activities and who respond positively to challenges rather than feeling overwhelmed by them. But they seem to be able to recognize the insidious action of repetitive over-arousal before it affects their well-being. They also realize that there is no single solution to the problem of stress–after all, what is stressful for one person is not necessarily stressful for everyone–so the ultimate responsibility for our well-being rests first and foremost with ourselves.

In order to feel in control, we must develop a healthy, stress-proofed lifestyle. Over the past few years growing awareness of the importance of balanced nutrition, the need for exercise, the dangers of smoking, alcohol and drugs, and the hazards of environmental pollution and ecological imbalance, have fostered a renewed interest in holistic well-being. Not a new concept, it is based on the ancient Greek ideal of unity of the mind and

body. We cannot separate our physical health from
the well-being of our minds. Both are closely interdependent. In turn, equilibrium of both mind and
body is determined largely by the way we communicate
and relate to other individuals, and by the symbiotic
relationship between society and the environment.
Stress can arise in any area of life when we fail to
respect the interdependence of human beings and all
other living organisms or if we upset the rhythmic
balance of rest and movement, and the complementary
cycles of physical and mental activity, of work and
leisure activities.

The aim of this book is to encourage awareness of
this mind-body balance, and to foster more understanding of the relationship between ourselves and our
surroundings. On a practical level, the goal of each
chapter is to suggest different strategies and skills for
surviving stress in particular areas of life, and to inspire
new attitudes to familiar and diverse situations.

Adapting your lifestyle

You can apply these techniques of stress management
to every area of your life. After you have read the first
part of this book and learned how to assess your stress
levels and how they affect you, the second shows how
you can make changes in every area of your life so that
stressful situations are less likely to occur. It teaches
you how to be more confident and calm in yourself and
how to reduce stress in your personal relationships. It
also shows you how to make your working life less
stressful. At a time when high technology is
revolutionizing every aspect of the way we work, it has
become more essential than ever to humanize our
working environment and our professional relationships and to adopt more flexible attitudes to the structure of employment and our styles of working. Next
comes a chapter on time management, which gives a
range of hints about how to plan your days so that you
can fit in everything you want to do without running
out of time. Well organized people suffer fewer
pressures, scheduling their activities efficiently to
minimize the tyranny of "time stress". The following
chapter looks at the ways in which you can adapt your
home environment to make it more relaxing. And the
final chapter of this section covers nutrition and exercise, showing how your balance of energy intake and

consumption can have a profound effect on your stress level and your ability to cope with stress.

Most of the lifestyle changes outlined in the book are simple to implement–and you will probably find that you do some of them naturally anyway. But the majority of us have at least one aspect of our lifestyle that requires stress-proofing. Effective stress-management may simply mean making adjustments to your diet, such as reducing the amount of tea or coffee you drink–caffeine has a marked effect on the amount of adrenalin in the blood. Or it may be a matter of adopting one of the relaxation techniques described in the third section–systems such as yoga, meditation, and massage have a direct influence on relaxation, and also help you to develop a more positive, confident attitude to life's challenges. Alternatively, you may feel that you can rid yourself of accumulated nervous energy and tension by taking up more vigorous exercise, to give yourself a feeling of "release". In this case, you will also find suitable exercises in this part of the book–especially in the Body Management chapter.

Giving yourself a break
Allowing ourselves to become chronically overstressed is often a warning sign that we have stopped paying attention to who we really are. Yet ignoring our innermost needs invariably restricts our natural capacity for growth, and losing touch with our true feelings dulls our impulse for individual self-expression and limits our capacity to become happier, more fulfilled human beings. Having the courage to examine long-held beliefs, to challenge–and possibly change–your attitudes toward yourself, your work, and your relationships, may in turn alter your whole relationship to stress. Recognizing that you have a right to make mistakes, to refuse excessive demands, to say "no", to express your needs and feelings openly, to make time for yourself, and to cater for your wants as well as those of others –all these are central to cultivating a healthy, balanced sense of "self-altruism", probably the most basic survival skill of all. Learning to give yourself a break, in every sense of the word, takes practice, especially when you are the one who is driving yourself the hardest. But the rewards in terms of regaining self-possession, and restoring the feeling that you have control over your life, can prove incalculable.

HOW STRESSED
ARE YOU?

The causes of stress

Every day we face some sort of challenge. At home, at work, even at play, out-of-the ordinary demands are imposed on our minds and bodies. Stress is the state of arousal with which the body responds to such demands. We cannot live without stress, since we face these challenges all the time. And no matter how diverse the sources and variable the levels of stress we experience, the mechanism that registers arousal and helps us cope with all the challenges that we face is shared by the entire human race.

Our response to challenge is prompt, speedy, and efficient. When we first perceive the challenge a chain reaction of automatic bodily processes provides an instant surge of energy and strength, effectively preparing us to fight or to flee. Earlier in our evolutionary history, our ability to make use of this "fight or flight" response meant the difference between life and death. Even today, it is just as necessary in certain situations, enabling us to cope with extra demands to the best of our ability. The reflexes that prepare the mind and body to run a race, to perform in public, and to meet deadlines, are identical to those that enabled our early ancestors to deal with attacks from wild animals or invading tribes.

While the causes of stress are vastly changed, our primitive response to them remains unaltered. Civilization has created new pressures that test our ability to survive. We cannot deal with the common, everyday stress situations of the modern world through physical exertion. So our body's response to these challenges is often inappropriate. This is not harmful in itself, provided that we can discharge the energy and tension that are generated through the fight or flight response. But often, when we are faced with repeated, persistent situations that unconsciously arouse the body, energy builds up but is not used. Physical pressure accumulates and can eventually lead to exhaustion and disease. In order to avoid this situation, we must learn either to release the pressure (for example, by exercising), or to "turn off" the arousal response by adopting a conscious relaxation technique.

The stage at which manageable, positive arousal turns into unhealthy over-stress is different for all of us. Our personality, behaviour, and lifestyle all have important influences on our stress level. Much stress occurs through emotions such as aggression, impatience, anger, anxiety, and fear, all of which kindle the body's stress responses. Eating an unhealthy diet, smoking, drinking, and taking drugs can also contribute further to physical strain. Stress may be generated through work, at home, within relationships, as a result of internal emotional conflict, through environment, diet, ill health, and financial insecurity as well as through major life events–from childbirth to bereavement, marriage to divorce.

Above all, stress is what we perceive it to be. Some people may thrive on a particular situation, while others may find it terrifying and highly stressful. Too little stimulus can be as stressful as too much. But stress only becomes harmful when we cannot control our responses to it. Recognizing this fact is the vital first step to reducing the harmful effects of stress in your life.

The fight or flight response

Popularly labelled the "fight or flight response" the body's answer to challenge or danger consists of a complex chain of bodily and biochemical changes involving the interaction of the brain, the nervous system, and a variety of different hormones. As a result of this the body goes on "full alert". Whether we are faced with a life-threatening situation or whether we are about to run a race or meet a deadline, we have all the available energy to respond to the challenge. In response to stress chemicals such as adrenalin, increased blood pressure, heart rate, oxygen intake, and blood flow to the muscles, combine to provide us with the strength, energy, and clear thinking necessary if we are to give of our best. Other parts of the body are also affected by the response. The digestive system shuts down (explaining why stress can lead to ulcers); the skin sweats; and the muscles tense up in preparation for action.

Measuring the arousal response

The heart and blood vessels play a major role in arousal, so the arousal level can be gauged by measuring the heart rate. A fit man with a healthy resting heart rate of around 60-75 beats per minute could find his maximum heart rate rapidly rising and levelling out at 190-220 beats per minute when the sympathetic branch of his nervous system responds to the challenge of running a race. When the challenge has been fully met, the parasympathetic branch of the autonomic nervous system takes over, allowing all organs to relax and regenerate, and the heart rate returns to normal. The lower the heart's resting rate, the more efficiently it can cope with extra demands.

AROUSAL AND RECOVERY

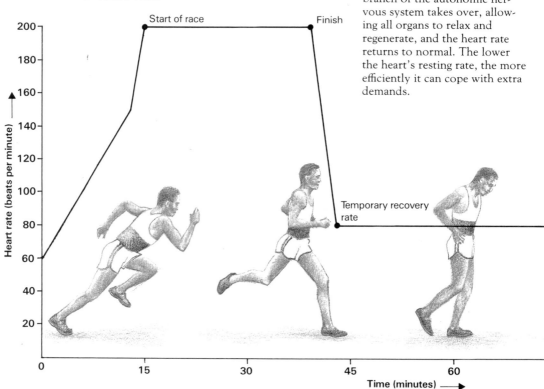

The body's response

Arousal is triggered initially in the hypothalamus (a tiny cluster of cells at the base of the brain), which controls all automatic body functions. Here a complex chain reaction of nerve and chemical impulses activates the sympathetic branch of the autonomic nervous system which results in a number of changes throughout the body.

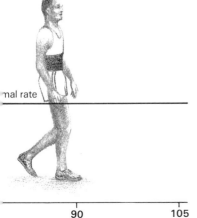

nal rate

90   105

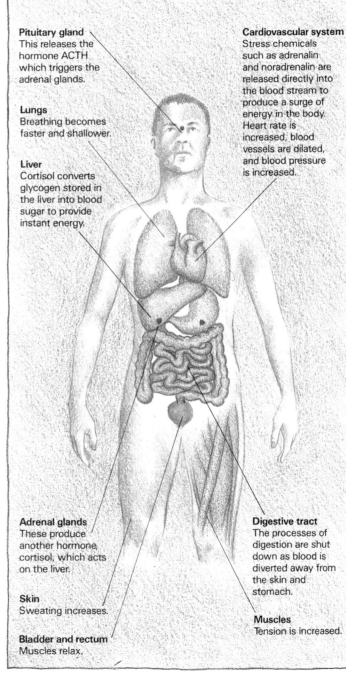

THE BODY'S AROUSAL RESPONSE

Pituitary gland
This releases the hormone ACTH which triggers the adrenal glands.

Lungs
Breathing becomes faster and shallower.

Liver
Cortisol converts glycogen stored in the liver into blood sugar to provide instant energy.

Cardiovascular system
Stress chemicals such as adrenalin and noradrenalin are released directly into the blood stream to produce a surge of energy in the body. Heart rate is increased, blood vessels are dilated, and blood pressure is increased.

Adrenal glands
These produce another hormone, cortisol, which acts on the liver.

Skin
Sweating increases.

Bladder and rectum
Muscles relax.

Digestive tract
The processes of digestion are shut down as blood is diverted away from the skin and stomach.

Muscles
Tension is increased.

The production of stress

Because the autonomic nervous system cannot differentiate between the various sources of arousal to which we are subjected, so our body's response is identical whether we are faced with the stress of being caught in a traffic jam or being chased by a mad bull. The fight or flight response to stress is perfectly healthy provided it is merited in the first place and we can use the energy it creates, as we would when running away from the bull. But when it is inappropriate or kept up for too long it may start to generate harmful stress and nervous tension. When this happens, what began as a normal and positive set of reflexes assisting healthy bodily function instead becomes unhealthy and counterproductive. If it continues to happen over a long period of time, it can become a cause of serious illness.

Recent research into the interaction between mind and body shows that we may place our body on stress "alert" quite unconsciously because of our psychological and emotional attitudes to stress. Anticipatory emotions like impatience, anxiety, anger, and fear can produce the same nerve impulses and chemical reactions as being faced with a concrete challenge. The hypothalamus is tuned to incoming messages from various parts of the brain. So it continues to prepare the body for action in anticipation, even if that action never takes place, allowing undischarged stress chemicals and muscular tension to build up. In addition, if you are a "stress addict", hooked on your own level of stress chemicals such as noradrenalin, feeling "high" and energetic may cause you unconsciously to seek further sources of arousal.

The fight or flight response diminishes as the source of stress is removed or resolved. So when faced with a stressful situation, we must either use up the energy created by the fight or flight response, or learn how to "turn off" the response using a conscious relaxation exercise or technique. Only then can the body relax again, as the heart rate, blood pressure, oxygen consumption, and muscle tension all drop to their normal levels, and new blood flows to the muscles, the inner organs, and the skin. With this switch from arousal to relaxation, the organs of the body can regenerate and function normally once more.

Finding a way of using up accumulated energy is usually a good way to banish tension. Afterwards you will feel much more able to relax.

The stress response

The initial stage of arousal remains the same whether you are faced with a major or minor challenge. But under extreme, prolonged, or persistent pressure the body continues to manufacture extra quantities of stress chemicals, triggering further processes to maintain energy. If arousal continues, the adrenal glands manufacture anti-inflammatory chemicals that simultaneously speed tissue repair while depressing the body's immune defence system. If all these changes continue, the body goes on trying to adapt under increasing strain and pressure. Eventually it breaks down. Exhaustion, a variety of illnesses–and even death–may be the outcome of uninterrupted, excessive stress.

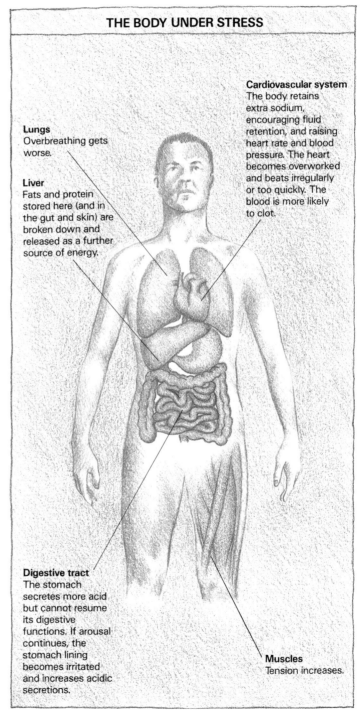

THE BODY UNDER STRESS

Lungs
Overbreathing gets worse.

Liver
Fats and protein stored here (and in the gut and skin) are broken down and released as a further source of energy.

Cardiovascular system
The body retains extra sodium, encouraging fluid retention, and raising heart rate and blood pressure. The heart becomes overworked and beats irregularly or too quickly. The blood is more likely to clot.

Digestive tract
The stomach secretes more acid but cannot resume its digestive functions. If arousal continues, the stomach lining becomes irritated and increases acidic secretions.

Muscles
Tension increases.

Stress and personality

Personality is the most important influence on the way
we respond to all events and situations. The values,
attitudes, and behaviour patterns that make up our
uniqueness as individuals ultimately make us more or
less vulnerable to stress. The most deep-rooted com-
ponent of personality is your value system. This
reflects how you rate yourself in relation to others–and
how you see the world in general. Learned at a very
early age from those closest to you, it is likely to be the
most rigid, least flexible aspect of your personality.
Behaviour is the direct expression of these values and
attitudes, and reflects your innermost attitude to yourself. So the origin of much personal stress lies within
your perception or concept of yourself. Low self-
esteem can lead to a number of stress-inducing
problems: inability to adapt, willingness to place ex-
cessively high demands on yourself, and lack of assertiveness. It can also lead to poor self-expression, so
that you harbour negative emotions such as anger, fear,
aggression, and anxiety, rather than giving vent to
them. But you *can* alter your view of yourself. Just
how much depends on your ability to recognize the
behaviour patterns and facets of your personality that
may be holding you back.

Personality types

Psychologists have identified two broad personality
types, one of which is more prone to stress than the
other. "Type A" is the notorious stress-prone personality whose typical behaviour and lifestyle constantly elicit physical arousal. Type A's are impatient, ambitious, competitive, aggressive, and hard-working; they
set high goals and demands of themselves and others;
and they are particularly prone to stress-inducing
anticipatory emotions such as anxiety. "Type B's", on
the other hand, have a reverse profile. They are equ-
able, calm, relaxed, not overtly ambitious, and less at
risk from stress and heart disease. Few of us possess
all the characteristics of either type. In general our personality is made up of a preponderance of one or other
patterns of behaviour, or, in rare cases, a perfect
balance of both. Recognizing situations when our
stress-prone traits emerge helps protect us from stress.

*Many of the personality
traits that shape our
attitude to stress develop
at a very early age.*

Stress and lifestyle

Virtually everything in life is potentially stressful to
someone. Whether you allow a situation to affect you
adversely depends largely on your appraisal and ability
to control it. Unavoidable major life crises face us all
some time or another: divorce, separation, bereavement, examinations, financial struggles, and family conflict. But in additon to these events, there are many
other potential sources of stress that are dictated by
your own particular lifestyle. These can be far less obvious than the major life-crises, but can have a
cumulative, pervasive effect. If you work in a large,
crowded city, pursue a demanding and competitive job,
and have to battle with the noise and discomfort of
daily commuting, you face more potential stresses than
a happily married person living quietly in a small
country village. The factor that determines how these
affect you is how content and satisfied you are with
your lifestyle. Stress is more likely to occur if you find
yourself caught against your will in a certain way of life
or if you cannot shape and amend your lifestyle to suit
your needs.

Life's key stress points

There are certain areas of our
lives where stress is likely to be
a particular problem. These
broad categories are changes in
your lifestyle, challenges
associated with your performance (especially at work),
emotions such as anxiety and
fear, boredom, and the grief
associated with bereavement or
separation. It is worthwhile
being aware of these areas, so
that you can prepare yourself
for crises centering on these
problems and emotions.

STRESS POINTS

Change
Inflexible attitudes, adherance
to strict values and routines, as
well as fear of the unknown,
can create undue stress when
change challenges you to take
risks and be adaptable. The
better your health, the easier it
will be to cope.

Performance
We often thrive on stress
connected with the challenge
of physical performance or a
test of our skills. This is
healthy, provided that you
remain confident, and use up
the energy and tension
generated by extra demands.

Anxiety and fear
Negative anticipatory emotions
may prolong or amplify the
arousal caused by actual

events. They may also gear you
up to confront situations that
never occur. Psychological
stress can build up and affect
physical well-being.

Boredom
Lack of stimulus or interest at
work, unemployment, or
retirement may create
depression, apathy, and stress.
Doubts as to whether you are
needed or valued can lead to a
poor self-image and a sense of
alienation.

Grief
Bereavement or loss of a
partner through divorce or
separation can have a deep,
prolonged psychological effect.
If grief and anguish remain
unresolved, suppressed, or
unrecognized they can trigger
mental or physical breakdown.

The social readjustment scale

Health and survival are based on the body's ability to maintain a balance of all the physical and mental processes. This state of equilibrium is called homeostasis. Bodily arousal is an integral part of the body's general adaptation system through which it adjusts to change and tries to restore homeostasis. Too much change in our lives can overtax our adaptive resources causing illness. The Social Readjustment Ratings Scale, devised by the American doctors T. H. Holmes and R. H. Rahe, cites 41 positive and negative life events valued according to the amount of adjustment needed to cope with them.

Using the Holmes-Rahe scale
Scoring over 300 points in one year greatly increases the risk of illness, 150-299 reduces the risk by 30 per cent, while a score of less than 150 involves a slight chance of illness. But illness is not an inevitable result of change. Your personality and your ability to cope largely determine how well you react.

THE HOLMES RAHE SCALE	
Life event	Lifechange units
Death of spouse	100
Divorce	73
Marital separation	65
Imprisonment	63
Death of close family member	63
Personal injury or illness	53
Marriage	50
Dismissal from work	47
Marital reconciliation	45
Retirement	45
Change in health of family member	44
Pregnancy	40
Sexual difficulties	39
Gain of new family member	39
Business readjustment	39
Change in financial state	38
Change in number of arguments with spouse	35
Major mortgage	32
Foreclosure of mortgage or loan	30
Change in responsibilities at work	29
Son or daughter leaving home	29
Trouble with in-laws	29
Outstanding personal achievement	28
Spouse begins or stops work	26
Begin or end school	26
Change in living conditions	25
Revision of personal habits	24
Trouble with boss	23
Change in work hours or conditions	20
Change in residence	20
Change in schools	20
Change in recreation	19
Change in church activities	19
Change in social activities	18
Minor mortgage or loan	17
Change in sleeping habits	16
Change in number of family reunions	15
Change in eating habits	15
Vacation	13
Christmas	12
Minor violation of the law	11

Environmental and chemical causes

Cramped or inadequate housing, violence, noise, crowding, and pollution are the most obvious sources of environmental stress. The larger a town or city, the more pervasive and uncontrollable the irritations and pressures that confront its inhabitants. The intensity of these stress factors and how many combine together depends on the areas in which you live and work, the type of transport you use, and whether you can get away from your environment occasionally.

Personality is often a decisive factor in how you react to environmental pressures–whether you are turned on or brought down by them. Competitive, ambitious, type A people tend to seek out and thrive on the energy and pace of big cities. They might dismiss as boring and irritating the quietness and slower pace of rural or suburban life that appeals to the calmer type B personality. You will probably minimize environmental stress if you live and work in the type of environment that allows you to feel and function at your best.

Life's discomforts

City people are continuously bombarded by irritations, a broad spectrum of diverse stress factors. Cramped living conditions that inhibit privacy and ugly, impersonal high-rise dwellings that cause loneliness and isolation are often responsible both for domestic stress and mental illness. Dirt, smells, chemical pollution from petrol exhaust, and cigarette smoke can be equally stressful, but easier to overcome. Crowding in public transport, shopping centres and other public places can become less stressful if you manage to relax and mentally transcend the relentless crush and aggressive jostling crowds. By far the most pervasive stress factor is noise. Whether the mind blocks it or not, the body reacts to noise by arousing the sympathetic nervous system, bringing the stress response into play. Over long periods a constant background of unremitting noise can impair your ability to concentrate, affecting learning skills.

But beware of tricking yourself into thinking that you are performing your best in a particular environment when you are not. Many people enjoy city life without realizing the stresses and strains it creates. If

Urban crowding– especially on cramped public transport–is a major stress factor in modern life.

you do not adjust to it, or compensate for it, the pace of city life can ultimately prove stressful even if you enjoy it most of the time. But there are ways of lessening the stress of the city without moving away from it. For example, altering your schedule (see pp. 76-81), can be an excellent way of avoiding the noise and crowds of the city. Alternatively, you can try a different type of work if this is possible–for example, working from home or doing a job that is closer to your home, to minimize the stresses of travelling (see pp. 66-9).

Chemical causes of stress

Chemicals in the atmosphere are not the only substances in our environment that can be causes of harmful stress. Some of the most destructive substances actually form part of our diet. The chemicals in many of our foods, drinks, and drugs contribute to stress.

Caffeine and other stimulants in coffee, tea, and cola drinks boost the output of stress hormones. The initial effect is to make us more alert. But it is not long before these substances cause feelings of irritability, while they can also cause sleeplessness. Eating large quantities of sugar and sugar-rich foods may lead to low blood sugar (the condition known to doctors as hypoglycaemia), which is another cause of fatigue and irritability. Salt increases nervous tension, fluid retention, and blood pressure.

Nicotine in cigarettes directly stimulates the adrenal glands causing a full stress response. Alcohol in moderation helps the body and mind relax, but taken in excess it acts as a depressant, damaging the liver, and impairing brain and sensory function. Hyperactivity in some children may be linked to food additives.

The answer to all these potential problems is to assess their importance in your life (see pp. 38-44) and, if necessary, alter your lifestyle so that their effects are minimized. The most obvious changes to make are in your diet (see pp. 92-5) but there are other areas where you can eliminate chemical stress factors. Check the toxic effects of any chemicals you use at work–and remember that offices can be as vulnerable as factories: carbonless copying paper is one material that should be kept carefully in a sealed container.

Many drugs and foods can exacerbate stress if taken to excess. Moderation is the best rule if you are in doubt about your diet.

Stress and you

Before you can cope with stress effectively, you must become aware of your own stress responses. This is not as straightforward as it sounds. The effects of stress are insidious and we often fail to notice them. Both the mind and body have a tremendous capacity for adaptation. The more readily we appear to adapt to the pressures around us, the greater the temptation to drive ourselves harder, beyond our capabilities. Stress distorts our perception, so that we do not notice that this is happening. If we allow the process to continue the result can be fatigue, exhaustion, and even, eventually, collapse. The more stressed we are, the less chance we have of realizing it, so it is vital to make ourselves aware of our stress responses.

There are two distinct types of personality who run the risk of health damage through their responses to stress. "Type A" people (see p. 24) rarely pause long enough to ponder the effects stress is having on them. In fact, they thrive on stress, probably because their bodies manufacture greater quantities than normal of noradrenalin, the stress hormone associated with feelings of confidence and elation. The mental and physical "high" produced by noradrenalin leads to what doctors term "stress addiction", and the addict purposely seeks out high-stress situations and indulges in stress-inducing behaviour. These people are not only hooked on stress–they are victimized by their own responses.

Just as much at risk from stress-related illnesses are "overachievers". Quieter, less obviously hyperactive than type A's, overachievers tend to accept life's pressures stoically. Dependable, cheerful, and seemingly always able to cope, they refuse to give in to illness or fatigue and cannot refuse excessive demands made on them. Perfectionists by nature, they are often driven by fear of falling short of their own expectations of themselves. They also tend to place the needs of others before their own and can find it hard to express their deepest feelings. They deny the possible dangers of stress and are unable accurately to assess personal limitations and admit vulnerability.

Many people combine some of the qualities of both these personality types. They may accept stress-related symptoms as a normal and inevitable part of life–until their health is affected. The principal way we can guard against becoming ill through too much stress is to recognize the early signals and know how far we can push ourselves without incurring the more serious symptoms. This means being more sensitive to your bodily functions and emotions on a very subtle level and looking out for all the signs and symptoms as soon as they occur.

This chapter is not intended to offer specific remedies for stress-related illnesses. If you do become ill, look at the remedies listed in Chapter 15, or consult your physician. But by learning, through the help of the following pages, to identify the signs and signals of stress, you should be able to recognize your own personal stress profile so that you can act before the major illnesses take hold. At the end of the chapter, a set of six questionnaires about various different aspects of your lifestyle directs you to the parts of the book most relevant to solving your particular stress problems.

Signals of tension

The human body is superbly equipped to deal with
stress–but only up to a certain level. If your adaptive
resources become overworked and exhausted your
body ceases to function smoothly. Different organs can
become stress targets. Symptoms may arise individually
in various combinations. Chronic stomach upsets,
headaches, skin rashes, backpain, irregular breathing
patterns, and sleeplessness, are common early indi-
cations that we are pushing ourselves too hard.
Psychological symptoms tend to creep up on us more
slowly and may be less easy to identify. Behaviour is a
prime giveaway of tension. Less noticeable to ourselves, it is those who are close to us who may be the
first to read these behavioural signals. Erratic,
uncharacteristic behaviour and mood swings often have
their origin in tension. Take all these signals
seriously–ignoring them can make them get worse.

Physical signals
The body transmits stress through various channels.
Unconscious, nervous reflexes (see right) lead to overt
physical stress signals. Many of these are lifetime
habits acquired during childhood. But we may be
more prone to them under stress. More serious signals
come in the form of physical stress-related illnesses (see
right). These vary according to which organ or system
is the weakest link in our physiological make-up.

Mood signals
Stress affects our mood in a variety of ways. Some
mood changes take place on the surface, while others
are deeper and more pervasive. Irritability and
impatience are hyperactive states, relatively superficial
manifestations of underlying anxiety and aggression.
Restlessness and frustration, if persistent, can be more
serious, developing into full-blown hostility or anger.
This can often be caused through lack of control or
fulfillment at work. Apathy and boredom are "flat"
feelings, often associated with low stimulus. They can
be just as stressful as more obviously stressed
emotions. Most serious are the "down" emotions,
such as guilt, shame, and the sense of helplessness or
hopelessness, as well as depression and fatigue, which

*The human body registers
stress in a number of
places, especially on the
head and feet. Habitually
touching the hair, ears, or
nose, grinding the teeth,
and biting the lips are
common signals, as are
foot tapping and turning.
(See the chart on the
opposite page for further
signals.)*

are often linked. If longlasting and severe, a downward, negative mood slide indicates more serious
underlying psychological problems.

Behavioural signals

Any behaviour which indicates that you are not acting
your usual self may be a sign of adverse reaction to
stress. Characteristic "type A" behaviour patterns
include leaving important tasks undone until the very
last minute then panicking and being unable to
complete them; allowing insufficient time to get to
work and to important appointments; trying to do two
or more things at the same time; and eating while
working. Stressed behaviour can impair our ability to
communicate well. Talking too fast, too loud, or too
aggressively, swearing, interrupting others or talking
over them, not listening to what people have to say,
and arguing for the sake of it, are typical ways in which
stress alters our way of relating to other people.
Nodding off during meetings or social gatherings, trying
to do without sleep, losing your sense of humour,
moving in a tense jerky way, and reacting nervously or
irritably to everyday sounds are other signs.

Outbursts and overreactions can occur when we lose
our perspective on problems that we would normally
face with equanimity. We lose our ability to
discriminate and judge even everyday situations or
events accurately, to control our reactions, and to cope
calmly. The occasional outburst, whether of anger or
of tears, may be a valid, healthy way to release pent-up
tension. But if repeated over a long period, overreac-
tive behaviour may indicate serious problems.

Consistently acting and feeling out-of-character is a
serious warning that we are losing our ability to cope
with tension. Inability to feel or express any emotions
or a sense of being "on automatic pilot", acting more
like a robot than a human being, indicates loss of contact with our surroundings and ourselves. Common
symptoms include: the inability to make decisions;
mind changes; memory blocks; loss of short-term
memory; being lost for words; and lapses of concentration. Inhibitions and anxiety when we are faced with
everyday challenges are further symptoms.

STRESS SIGNALS

Nervous reflexes
Biting nails, clenching fists,
clenching jaw, drumming fingers,
grinding teeth, hunching
shoulders, picking at facial skin,
picking at skin around
fingernails, tapping feet,
touching hair.

Stress-related illnesses
Asthma, back pain, digestive
disorders, headaches, migraines,
muscular aches and pains,
sexual disorders, skin disorders.

Mood changes
Anxiety, depression, frustration,
habitual anger or hostility,
helplessness, hopelessness,
impatience, irritability,
restlessness.

Behaviour
Aggression, disturbed sleep
patterns, doing several things at
once, emotional outbursts,
leaving jobs undone,
overreactions, talking too fast or
too loud.

*This chart lists some of the
most common signs of
stress. In addition, any
behaviour or mood that is
unusual for the person
concerned is likely to be a
signal of tension.*

Emotional props

There are times when we all need to call on extra
sources of help and support to back up our own
resources. The danger lies in using "emotional props"
as substitutes for this sort of support, and becoming
over-reliant on them. Dependence on drugs, cigarettes,
alcohol, and certain "comfort" foods, can lead to addiction and ill-health. By contrast, the support you get
from your partner, family, and close friends can
provide a positive and nurturing force in your life.

True supports

The back-up, encouragement and advice we get from
people who are close to us, and whose opinion and
judgment we respect, is the most valuable support of
all. The relationships between yourself and your
partner, family, and close friends, should be based on a
fair balance of give and take. Support is a reciprocal,
two-way affair. Mutual trust, respect, loyalty, affection,
and love are the qualities that constitute the most
enduring, mutually supportive friendships.

False props

Alcohol taken in moderation helps us relax. But
there is a narrow dividing line between drinking for
enjoyment and through choice and doing so compul-
sively because we feel we need alcohol to help us
escape or cope with our problems, or to function well.
Of course, alcohol taken to excess does not allow you
to function efficiently, and can only lead to impaired
performance, increasing dependency, alcoholism, and,
ultimately, serious health damage. The same obviously
applies to "hard" drugs like cocaine and heroin. But
these are not the only drugs to be wary of. Addiction
to tranquillizers, anti-depressants, and sleeping pills is
one of the most serious problems facing many people
who are overstressed. The action of these drugs is
insidious, the effects all-pervasive. As you increase the
dosage you lose touch with your real emotions, becoming
unaware of the true cause of your problem. Taking
them over long periods impairs your ability to think,
act, and behave normally. If you think you are in
danger of becoming addicted to hard drugs, alcohol, or
tranquillizers, seek professional help immediately.

*The sympathy of another
person is the best form of
support we can receive in
times of trouble or tension.*

Acute crisis effects

The amount and type of stress we can cope with before damaging our health varies for everyone. But we all have a crisis point, beyond which we can become seriously ill. A build-up of long-term pressures can lead to the relentless, accumulated strain that results in this crisis. Fortunately, most of us manage to recognize the warning signs before it is too late. Friends, family, or your doctor or counsellor may notice the signs before you do and can help you break out of the stress spiral before your health and performance are seriously impaired. Acute crisis effects take on very definite characteristics–they are not always obvious to the sufferer and the difficulty lies in being able to notice them and accept them as deviations from the norm.

Breakdown

Under healthy pressure, arousal leads to an automatic increase in performance, followed by a healthy fatigue which we remove by resting. In the case of repeated, unrelenting pressures, arousal persists but our performance falls far short of the intended mark. As we push ourselves even harder to attain our goal, we are caught in a self-defeating struggle to close the gap between what we are capable of achieving and what we think we should achieve. Greater arousal depletes our resources to the point where any further demand may lead to a breakdown. Among the many symptoms of arousal and unhealthy fatigue the most common are: disturbed sleep patterns, chronic tiredness, loss of energy and judgment, overdependence on alcohol and drugs, eating disorders including anorexia and bulimia, hyperventilation, and panic attacks. People suffering from a breakdown may also display neurotic, manic or depressive behaviour, and will probably deny that their performance is impaired by the breakdown.

The symptoms of breakdown

The causes of physical breakdown can range from heart attack, angina, and stroke, to kidney disease, viral infection, stomach and respiratory disorders. The term "nervous breakdown" is something of a misnomer: our nerves cannot literally break down. Any behaviour which is uncharacteristic, uncontrollable, and irrational,

PANIC ATTACKS AND RECOVERY

Panic

The acute crisis effects of stress may show themselves in the form of a panic attack, in which your fear intensifies so that you feel out of control. Physical symptoms, particularly difficulty in breathing, are also severe.

Recovery

First, remember that however frightened you feel, the attack will not harm you permanently and will pass. Do not try to fight the feeling — this will only make it worse. Use the "stop" relaxation exercise. Sit down calmly at a table, putting your hands firmly on the table. Say "stop" loudly. Keep your knees uncrossed, your body relaxed, and breathe slowly and rhythmically. Focus on any object in the room; look at it carefully and lose yourself in all its details. Describe it over and over to yourself until you are lost in thought. Carry on until you feel calm and balanced.

Back-up

If you are prone to panic attacks, read the chapters on The Art of Being (pp. 46-63), Relaxation Techniques (pp. 100-13), and Breathing (pp. 126-31), for more information on ways to relax.

although perceived as quite normal by the person displaying it, usually indicates a severe psychological disorder. Severe mental strain can for example cause prolonged bouts of sobbing, screaming, shouting, physical violence, self-mutilation, or even attempted suicide. Hyperventilation can become extreme, triggering acute and crippling panic attacks that mimic the symptoms of a heart attack or stroke. There are also a number of behavioural symptoms that may indicate this type of breakdown. Suddenly resigning from one's job or ending a close relationship; running away from home; abandoning one's children; shoplifting; becoming completely dependent on hard drugs or alcohol; and developing a "split" personality are among the most serious. Such symptoms are likely to require instant medical treatment. Removal of the sources of stress, enforced rest and sleep, short-term drug therapy, and psychotherapy usually cause the symptoms of breakdown to improve, encouraging renewed well-being on both physical and mental levels.

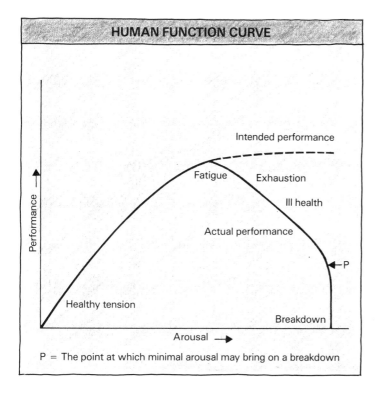

HUMAN FUNCTION CURVE

Intended performance

Fatigue Exhaustion

Ill health

Actual performance

Performance

←P

Healthy tension

Breakdown

Arousal →

P = The point at which minimal arousal may bring on a breakdown

The human function curve was devised by Dr Peter Nixon, consultant cardiologist at London's Charing Cross Hospital. It shows how performance initially increases with arousal, but declines if we carry on pushing ourselves after fatigue has set in. If this process is allowed to continue, ill health and breakdown may result. But we may not be aware of this, believing that our performance is still at the intended level (the broken line on the graph).

Assessing the stress in your life

The questionnaires on the following pages are designed to help you pinpoint the areas of your life where stress is occurring. Each question is accompanied by a cross-reference to the part of the book that is most relevant. As you ask yourself each question, bear in mind that there are usually ways of putting a situation right by changing external factors, but that there are also factors within the self that can cause stress. So remember these two groups of factors as you read through the questions. If you have an overwhelming feeling of negative emotion that does not seem to be focused on any particular area of your life, you will probably find it useful to read the entries on depression and panic attacks and anxiety in Chapter 15 (p. 177) for emergency and long-term remedies, and the whole of Chapter 3 (pp. 46–53) for further long-term suggestions.

Note *Accumulated stress can sometimes lead to generalized emotions of fear, anxiety, or depression, which are difficult to attribute to any single cause. If you are prone to these feelings or to panic attacks, turn to p. 177 for emergency and long-term help.*

YOUR ENVIRONMENT	
Do you never seem to have enough room to put things?	Adapting space, pp. 84–5
Is your home too small and cramped?	Adapting space, pp. 84–5 Architectural space, p. 85
Do you need more space at home in which to work?	Adapting space, pp. 84–5
Do you feel that you don't have enough privacy?	Personal space, pp. 84–5
Do you find it difficult to relax at home in the evenings?	Creating comfort, p. 86 Light and air, p. 88 Furniture and health, p. 89
Are your neighbours too noisy?	Noise, p. 185
Do you feel depressed in the dark winter months?	Light and air, p. 88 Depression, p. 177
Do you wake up in the morning with a stiff back?	Furniture and health, p. 89 Backache, p. 172
Do you feel uncomfortable after sitting for a long period?	Furniture and health, p. 89

YOURSELF

Do you feel trapped in a set of circumstances you cannot change?	Assuming control, p. 49 Growth and change, pp. 50–3
Do you feel you have many faults and few good points?	Being yourself, pp. 48–9
Do you feel anxious about talking to strangers?	Developing assertiveness, pp. 52–3 Talking, p. 70
Do you often suppress your own views because you think other people will be offended?	Developing assertiveness, pp. 52–3 Talking, p. 70
Do you often give up something you want to do because of what other people want?	Developing assertiveness, pp. 52–3 Families and groups, pp. 60–3
Do you find it difficult to talk about your problems?	Developing assertiveness, pp. 52–3 Conflicts and communication, pp. 56–7 Talking, p. 70
Do you often put off doing things until the last minute because you are anxious about the difficulties involved?	Developing assertiveness, pp. 52–3 Meeting challenges, pp. 72–3 Organizing time, pp. 78–9
Do you panic easily when faced with a difficult situation?	Calming down, pp. 48–9 Meeting challenges, pp. 72–3
Do you spend a lot of time worrying about the future?	Assuming control, p. 49 Anxiety and panic attacks, p. 177
Do you lose your temper easily?	Calming down, pp. 48–9
Do you burst into tears at the slightest provocation?	Calming down, pp. 48–9 Anxiety and panic attacks, p. 177
Do you feel guilty or depressed when you fail to reach your own targets or goals?	The art of being, p. 47
Do you find it difficult to relax?	Calming down, pp. 48–9 Inability to relax, p. 179 Relaxation and the body, p. 102 Choosing relaxation exercises, p. 103 Which exercise for you? pp. 96–8
Do you feel that your talents are very limited?	What can I do? p. 49
Do you find it difficult to prepare for the stressful times in your life?	Preparing for the stress points, pp. 57–8

YOUR RELATIONSHIPS

Do you feel you never have any time for yourself?	Analysing time, pp. 76–7 Developing assertiveness, pp. 52–3
Do you argue a lot about money?	Conflicts and communication, pp. 56–7 Money, p. 62 Marital rows, p. 181 Rows with children, p. 181
Do you feel that you don't have enough privacy at home?	Personal space, pp. 84–5
Do you feel guilty that you do not do more for your family?	Families and groups, pp. 60–3
Do you feel disappointed because your partner cannot live up to your ideal?	Couples, pp. 56–8
Are you finding it difficult to settle down into a permanent relationship?	Couples, pp. 56–8
Do you find it difficult to talk about sex with your partner?	Sex and stress, pp. 58–9
Do you feel that some of your sexual needs or preferences are abnormal?	Normality and you, p. 59
Do you often feel too tired to make love?	Normality and you, p. 59 Fatigue, p. 177 Inability to relax, p. 179
Is there ill-feeling in your family because some members never seem to pull their weight?	Giving, taking, and sharing, pp. 62–3
Do you find it a problem when children answer back or are rude to you?	Families and groups, p. 60 Developing assertiveness, pp. 52–3 Rows with children, p. 181
Are your family resentful that you don't spend enough time at home?	De-stressed schedules, pp. 80–1
Are you frustrated because you do not see enough of your friends?	De-stressed schedules, pp. 80–1 Groups outside the family, p. 63 Loneliness, p. 178
Do you feel resentful because your partner earns more than you?	Money, p. 62 Marital rows, p. 181 Job satisfaction, p. 68

YOUR JOB

Do you feel put-upon or feel you are working too hard?	Meeting challenges, p. 72 Overwork, p. 187
Do you regularly work during lunchtimes or evenings?	Organizing time, pp. 78–9 Overwork, p. 187
Do you never have holidays?	Organizing time, pp. 78–9
Are you depressed by your working environment?	The working environment, p. 69
Do you find it difficult to cope with a recent promotion?	Meeting challenges, p. 72
Do you feel unable to ask your boss for a rise or a holiday?	Developing assertiveness, pp. 52–3 Meeting challenges, p. 72
Do you feel bored with your job?	Routine and variety, p. 66
Do you find it difficult to organize your work, or are you required to do too many different things at once?	Organizing your work, pp. 66–7 Analysing your work, p. 73 Overwork, p. 187
Do you find it difficult to delegate work to someone else when you get busy?	Developing assertiveness, pp. 52–3
Do you find it difficult to get on with some of your colleagues?	Talking, p. 70 Meeting challenges, p. 72 Personality clash, p. 187
Do you think that communications channels are very poor at your place of work?	Solving communications problems, p. 70
Does your job involve the pressure of constant deadlines?	Organizing your work, pp. 66–7 Organizing time, pp. 78–9 Overwork, p. 187
Do you find that constant interruptions ruin your concentration?	Developing assertiveness, pp. 52–3
Do you work in a very noisy, stuffy, or smelly environment?	Combatting pollution at work, p. 69 Noise, p. 185 Smell, p. 185
Do you feel your talents or abilities are not fully recognized?	Developing assertiveness, pp. 52–3 Talking, p. 70
Do you have to work at relentless, mechanical tasks without the chance to rest?	Routine and variety, p. 66 Job satisfaction, p. 68

YOUR MANAGEMENT OF TIME

Do you usually try to do things as quickly as possible?	Personality types, p. 24 Planning your time, p. 75
Do you run out of time when working on important projects?	Organizing time, pp. 78–9
Do you deliberately try to do several things at once?	Organizing time, pp. 78–9 De-stressed schedules, pp. 80–1
Do you regularly forget about appointments or important deadlines?	Organizing time, pp. 78–9
Do you rarely plan any of your activities more than a day or two in advance?	Organizing time, pp. 78–9
Do you talk and walk quickly?	Personality types, p. 24
Do you get impatient easily?	Calming down, pp. 48–9 Assuming control, p. 49
Do you always feel in a hurry?	Organizing time, pp. 78–9
Do you feel that time is passing by too quickly?	Planning your time, p. 75
Does time spent travelling get you down?	De-stressed schedules, pp. 80–1
Do you always travel to work in the rush hour?	De-stressed schedules, pp. 80–1
Does your partner often get annoyed because you spend too much time working?	Conflicts and communication, pp. 56–7 Organizing your work, pp. 66–7 Analysing time, pp. 76–7
Do you only rarely give yourself a break to play, relax, laze, or day-dream?	Analysing time, pp. 76–7 Relaxation and the body, p. 102
Do you spend the majority of time with other people, with little time on your own?	Analysing time, pp. 76–7
Do you feel you spend too much time at home with the children?	Families and groups, pp. 60–3 Analysing time, pp. 76–7
Do you often lose your temper because there never seems to be enough time to finish what you need to do?	Calming down, pp. 48–9 Organizing your work, pp. 66–7 Organizing time, pp. 78–9 Irritability, p. 178
Do you never use a diary?	Organizing time, pp. 78–9

YOUR DIET AND EXERCISE

Do you regularly take less than half an hour for main meals?	The stress-free diet, pp. 94–5 De-stressed schedules, pp. 80–1
Do you often eat while you are doing other things, such as working, travelling, reading, cooking, or watching television?	The stress-free diet, pp. 94–5 De-stressed schedules, pp. 80–1
Do you eat a lot of high-calorie foods that produce an instant energy "high"?	Assessing your diet, pp. 92–3
Do you regularly eat any of the following: canned foods, refined foods, convenience foods, fatty or fried foods, vegetables that have been stored for long periods?	The stress-free diet, pp. 94–5
Do you drink more than five cups of tea or coffee a day?	Mood foods, p. 93
Do you drink more than 4 glasses of wine, 4 measures of spirits, or 2 pints of beer a day?	Emotional props, p. 34 Mood foods, p. 93 Dependence on alcohol, p. 178
Do you regularly have snacks between main meals?	The stress-free diet, pp. 94–5
Do you put on weight very easily or quickly?	Nutrition and exercise, p. 91 Which exercise for you? pp. 96–8 Overeating, p. 178
Do you get a lot of colds or virus infections?	Food supplements, p. 93 Common cold, p. 174
Do you smoke cigarettes?	Emotional props, p. 34 Cigarette smoking, p. 179
Do you never set aside some time every day for some form of conscious relaxation?	Relaxation and the body, p. 102 Choosing relaxation exercises, p. 103 Inability to relax, p. 179 Which exercise for you? pp. 96–8 Analysing time, pp. 78–9
Do you rarely allow yourself a rest period during the day?	De-stressed schedules, pp. 80–1
Do your daily activities rarely include some degree of physical exertion (such as walking briskly, chasing young children around, or doing moderate physical work)?	Body management, pp. 115–25

STRESS-PROOFING YOUR LIFESTYLE

The art of being

The way we see ourselves shapes everything we do. If you are self-confident and value yourself, you will feel that you are in control of your actions and your destiny. Stress is unlikely to be a major problem in your life if you feel this way. But if your confidence is low and you feel that you are not in control of your life, you are in danger of becoming a victim of persistent, overriding feelings of resentment, anxiety, and fear.

When life becomes intolerably stressful, the temptation is often to blame external influences. Obviously there are many outside influences on our lives, such as our personal relationships and what we do at work. But it is often we who are responsible for holding ourselves back from getting the most out of life and realizing our full potential. Even the way we communicate and relate to others is formed largely through our personal expectations and self-appraisal. Before we can form fulfilling, well balanced relationships we ourselves need to be fulfilled and well balanced. So we must learn to understand or accept yourself as you are, you may take on roles that are unsuited to

Know yourself. If you fail to understand or accept yourself as you are, you may take on roles that are unsuited to your true nature and needs. Perfectionists who set themselves impossibly high standards, or people who always put the needs of others first while denying their own, may be motivated more by a fear of failure or rejection than by true ambition or altruism.

Self-knowledge also involves recognizing the scope in your life for change and development. Contrary to what you may

feel, no one is completely trapped in the way they are now. We all have some choices about the way we look, move, speak, and conduct our daily lives and personal relationships. These can make a fundamental difference to the way we see ourselves. The actual process of change involves considerable courage and resolve, and it does not happen instantly. Most of us can gain or regain control of our actions and become stronger individuals once we recognize that habit is mainly to blame for the way we become trapped in false roles. You can overcome and reverse most of these patterns if you try hard enough, learning insight into your true self, and discovering which things you can change, which you cannot. This means assessing both your negative and positive qualities, accepting your faults as well as your strengths, and trying to achieve a balanced integration of both.

It is important to recognize, however, that change is not always an easy process and can sometimes even be painful. Shaking off the habits of a lifetime can be very difficult, especially when doing so involves being more assertive, or facing up to faults that you are unwilling to admit are your own. But the benefits of making these changes–greater confidence and self-esteem, and minimized stress–will compensate for the difficulties.

Don't set yourself up for disappointment by making impossible demands on yourself or others. Letting yourself off the hook and becoming more assertive can be difficult, but these skills will help you to develop the courage to stop striving to be what you are not and grow more successfully into what you are.

Being yourself

Everyone has good and bad points. Realizing that you are not perfect, that you are a normal human being, with insecurities and failings, is the first step to feeling good about yourself. If you have healthy self-esteem and a positive self-image you should be able to weigh up both your faults and your good points. If you find it difficult to assess your character in this way, enlist the help of a friend. Ask him or her to give you an honest character assessment, warts and all. Write down your good and bad qualities and acknowledge them. Be proud of your good points–the special capabilities and characteristics that make you uniquely you. But remember that some "good" qualities have their drawbacks: virtues like modesty and humility can be deterrents to establishing self-esteem.

One of the best methods for helping you to think positively about yourself is meditation. Visualization techniques can help you see yourself in the best possible light (see pp. 152-3).

Calming down

Mental calm and strength, the tranquil, quiet state that allows you to be perfectly centred, gives you more control over your thoughts and actions. When faced by a potentially stressful situation you will be aware of all the options open to you. If you are strong and calm, you can stand back, become more objective, and rationalize your feelings.

Tranquility may seem difficult to achieve if you are angry, frustrated, or afraid. But if you look upon these emotions as a normal part of life, and know what causes them, it will be easier to overcome them. Try to express your feelings openly whenever you can. If you do not, you may suppress them or drive them inward, directing them at yourself. By expressing them, you will be able to dissipate them quickly and completely.

Once you have learned to express them, get used to "dropping" destructive thoughts and feelings consciously before they start to build up. If you do this, you will learn to intercept your conditioned responses to stress. People vary in their preferred techniques for breaking conditioned stress patterns. Meditation (see pp. 147-53), hanging upside-down (see p. 112), or chant-

WHAT SORT OF PERSON AM I?	
Calm	Animated
Type A	Type B
Thoughtful	Impetuous
Intellectual	Practical
Leader	Follower
Conventional	Unconventional
Realistic	Idealistic
Solitary	Gregarious
Quiet	Talkative
City	Country
Religious	Agnostic

When you ask yourself what sort of person you are, think about character traits like these. You are unlikely to be wholly one extreme or the other–few people have characters that are made up entirely of extremes. Write down your profile and you will be able to see very easily your characteristics and abilities.

ing rhythmically are all good methods of calming down if you can escape to the appropriate place. Lying on the floor, concentrating on the weight of your limbs and the centering pull of gravity is also very calming. But other diversion exercises, which you can do sitting down, are just as effective. Sit down calmly, put your hands firmly on a table, and say "stop" loudly. Keep your knees uncrossed, your body relaxed, and breathe slowly and rhythmically. Focus your gaze on any object in your environment. It can be anything: your left thumb, a pencil, or a bowl of sugar. Observe all its aspects in minute detail. Become aware of its smell and texture. Lose yourself completely in it. Silently describe it and your relationship to it over and over to yourself until you are lost in a fantasy. After five minutes you should feel calm and balanced.

Assuming control

Even if you do not have much control over events that take place around you at work, at home, and in your relationships, you do have a choice as to how you react to them. Look for the positive aspects of any event or situation, no matter how stressful or unpleasant. Try to learn or gain something from the situation. You may feel trapped because you have not examined the choices you have of responding differently. Simply refusing to lose your temper, or to get tearful or worried can help you gain control. You should also examine your past patterns of reaction. Many of these may have become totally automatic and irrational. Anxiety, for example, is a rehearsal of a situation that will probably never happen. Our attitude to stress, not stress itself, can cause us to feel victimized.

Each time a stressful event occurs and you start getting anxious or losing your temper, give yourself a control test. Sit down on your own for a few minutes and make yourself aware of your pulse, breathing and muscle tension. Then hold your breath for ten seconds, and exhale loudly and explosively. Do this few times, then breathe normally and smile. As you gain control over your innermost responses you will be able to act more positively and you will find it easier to feel good about yourself.

WHAT CAN I DO?
Cook
Do accounts
Drive
Garden
Mend a fuse
Put up shelves
Type
Paint and draw
Play a musical instrument
Play a sport

If you find it hard to think positively about your character, list everything you can do—from the simplest thing to the most complicated. You may be surprised at the range of your abilities.

Growth and change

Social and environmental conditioning have a far-reaching influence on our characters. The attitudes we develop as we grow up may prevent us from assuming as much control over our lives as we would like. Though we may be aware of the various options and alternative choices open to us we may be inhibited from acting freely and positively, yet we cannot grow and change before first questioning the role we have chosen to play in life. Women, for example, are often conditioned to give unselfishly and suppress their own desires. Often the more they give, and deny their right to take, the more resentful they become, especially if they receive little appreciation in return. Fear of rejection when we state our needs, inability to express anger, and the need to obtain approval from others can all prevent us from being assertive enough to take control of our lives.   Another common problem is setting impossibly high standards for yourself and feeling guilty when you fail to reach your goal. So the first step toward real change depends upon challenging any assumptions and views about yourself that may be holding you back. The second lies in having both the determination and courage to make the necessary changes where possible. The third involves developing the skills of asssertiveness which can help you attain your goals and put you in control.

The power of change

Implementing even very minor or external changes can help to alter the way we feel about ourselves. For example, losing weight or changing the style of clothes that you wear may dramatically alter the way others perceive you, in turn boosting your own body image and self-esteem. There are many other areas where change is possible or desirable. Giving up cigarettes, drinking less alcohol, following a healthier diet, controlling habits such as nail-biting, tackling phobias, and taking up regular exercise or challenging new sports and activities–these will both improve your physical well-being and help you overcome fears and inhibitions.

Cast an honest, probing look at your life and actions and challenge your assumptions about yourself. Is

WHAT CAN I CHANGE?	
Home environment	**Personal appearance**
Lighting	Clothes
Ventilation	Hair
Furniture	Make-up
Colour scheme	Weight
Diet	**Leisure interests**
Sweet foods	Exercise
Fatty foods	Sport
Snacks	Meditation
Coffee	New hobbies

You may feel that there are few things in your life that you can change. But even if you cannot get a new job or move to a new home, there are things you can change–what you eat, how you look, what you do in your spare time. Some of these will compensate for other areas that cannot be changed–and prepare you for bigger changes that you can make later.

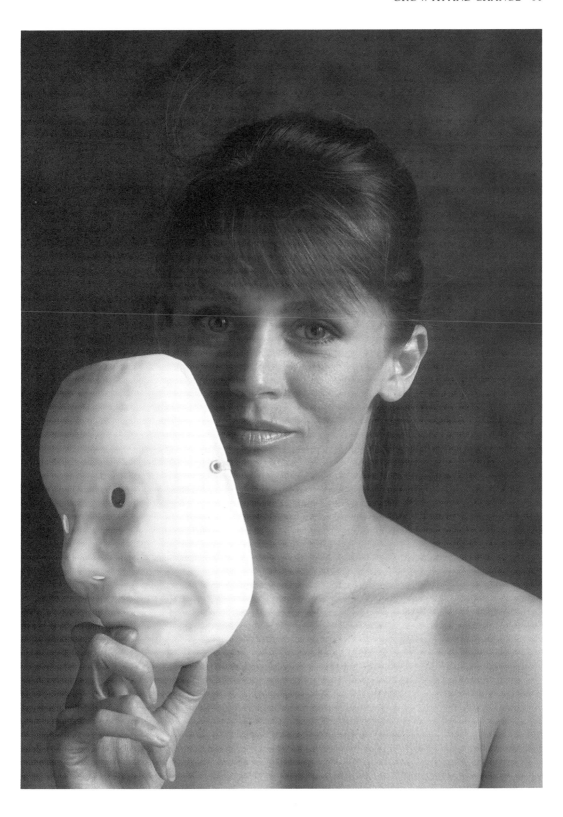

your job really the one you want or are you staying on out of habit? Fear of failing often stops us taking risks, whether this involves learning to ski, changing jobs, or getting out of a relationship. Are you trying to please people all the time? Knowing when and how to say "no" graciously but firmly suggests you know your own worth and capabilities. Do you feel guilty or inadeqate because you cannot meet your own very high standards? Try to be less of a perfectionist. Realizing that there are areas of your personality that can be changed for the better encourages you to take charge of your own well-being and to respect yourself a lot more. This sort of change is not always easy and you will often find yourself reverting to your original patterns of behaviour. But if you are persistent with yourself, new habits and types of behaviour will start to come more naturally, until they become second nature.

Developing bodily assertiveness

About 70 per cent of human communication is non-verbal. So your gestures, postures, and movements can be as powerful as words in getting your message across to others. The way you walk and stand gives a clear impression of how confident you are. A slouched stance, concave chest, and downward gaze convey lack of confidence and a desire to remain unnoticed. Standing tall, with your chest expanded, head held erect, and eyes level, implies you recognize your own strengths and capabilities. Walking with a relaxed, poised body, and a firm, rhythmic stride shows that you know where you are going but can get there at your own pace. Avoid obvious signs of nervousness and fear–hunched shoulders, clenched fists, tightly clasped hands, and a tapping foot. Sit upright, shoulders relaxed, hands at your sides or loosely clasped. Arms gently folded give an impression of ease and confidence. If you grip them too tightly you will appear hostile or aggressive. Using sharp "cutting" or "chopping" hand movements and drumming your fingers also conveys impatience and a closed mind. Turning the palms up-ward in a supplicatory gesture suggests passivity and quiescence. The way you look at others is also impor-tant. No matter how difficult it seems, you should al-

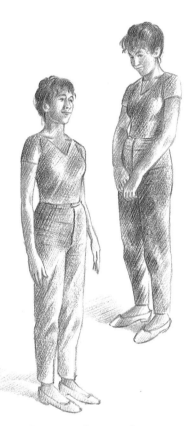

Posture is often a good indicator of how confident you are feeling. Standing tall (above left) gives a much better impression than slouching down (above right). What is more, adopting a confident posture will also help you feel more confident.

ways try to make eye contact with the people you are talking to–but do so without staring, which people usually interpret as a challenge. When you break eye contact don't look down, but maintain your basic eye level. Remember to keep your head level since tilting it sideways implies lack of resolve or ambivalence.

Developing verbal assertiveness

The words we use and our tone of voice can have a profound if unconscious effect on the listener. Gentle, unforced breathing and a relaxed jaw and facial muscles help to keep the voice's tone steady. Try not to talk too fast (which can be confusing) or pitch your voice too high (which can be irritating). Raising your voice in anger, interrupting others, and using threatening language are direct signs of aggression and lack of self-control–avoid them at all times. If you are shy, develop assertiveness by initiating daily greetings and conversations with people who are not close friends. Get used to giving compliments and accepting them politely when they are paid to you. Don't be afraid of using the word "I", and get used to stating as many opinions, even when you are not asked, as posing questions. When others disagree with what you have to say don't interpret this as a personal rejection–it usually isn't. Asking "why?" more frequently indicates that you want or need additional information. Provided you ask calmly and pleasantly, especially if you are talking to a superior at work, it will not come across as a threat or a challenge. Alternative queries such as "What makes you say that?" or "Could you explain a bit more?" may sound less threatening than a simple "Why?". Tell someone when you disagree with them, saying so quietly and firmly. Believe in what you say, and don't be arbitrary or ready to retract what you've said. Try to express your feelings directly and spontaneously, not days or weeks after the event or occasion that prompted them. The more you practise, the easier this should become. Try to be aware of irritating verbal mannerisms and unconscious habits such as coughing, sighing, sniffing, giggling, and using meaningless phrases like "you know", "sort of thing", "are you with me", or "yeah" frequently while you talk.

AM I ASSERTIVE ENOUGH?

Negative
I don't suppose you want to go to the movies tonight?

Positive
I'm going to a movie tonight — it would be nice if you come too.

Unspecific
You're always nagging me.

Specific
Last night you told me four times to do the washing up.

Unspecific
You never listen to what I'm saying.

Specific
I know a lot about running a business — next time you should listen to my opinion.

Unspecific
I'm so bored.

Specific
I feel bored when you say the same thing over and over again.

When it comes to being assertive the most important rules are to be positive and specific. If you are negative about what you are saying, people will not agree with you; if you are vague, or don't give examples of what you are talking about, people will not know what you mean.

The art of relating

A close and loving relationship is the most fundamental of all human needs. Our capacity for self-expression, and our happiness and emotional security depend closely on the way we relate to others. Few of us manage to live alone happily for any length of time unless we suppress many basic needs and desires.

Building long-lasting, happy relationships has become one of the major challenges of our age. The modern nuclear family, unlike the large families of the past, lacks the supportive network of sibling groups and neighbouring relatives. So it must depend far more on its own resources. Other styles of relationship–the homosexual couple, the single-parent family, and the "extended family" of several couples or individuals–also rely on strong internal resources for lasting success and fulfillment.

The changing social role of women has brought about profound changes in modern relationships. Women suffer stress as a result of working both in their job and at home (few husbands do their share of the housework). Working mothers suffer guilt about leaving their children to go out to work. Working not because you want to, but because you need to augment the family income also puts strains on your relationship with your partner and children. Men can fall prey to stress as a result of feeling undermined in their former role of breadwinner.

To make our relationships work we need to adapt to changing circumstances and to reassess the traditional guidelines and values in marriage. The expectations we have of ourselves, our partners, and of relationships in general are now far greater than they were in the past. Sexual satisfaction, emotional and intellectual fulfilment, and compatibility of interests, attitudes, and ambitions are what many of us search for in the ideal relationship. This motivates us to work at achieving richer, more fulfilling and equally balanced partnerships based as much on friendship and intellectual equality as on sexual attraction and romantic love. Yet it also makes us more critical and less tolerant when we fail to find satisfaction. Placing too many demands on our partner or having unrealistically high expectations of marriage is a root cause of domestic strife and marital breakdown. It is after all unrealistic to expect any one person to satisfy all of our needs and desires. Unless we can learn when and how to compromise we may place an intolerable strain on even the most loving and supportive of partners. The guilt and sense of inadequacy that stem from not being able to fulfil our partner's every want and need may in turn cause us strain and anguish.

Fortunately we possess excellent resources for making the best of our relationships. Frankness and honesty between the sexes have never been greater than they are today. We possess more freedom and greater resources to work at our relationships by openly expressing our needs, finding mutually acceptable areas of compromise, and achieving a fair balance of give and take. Using these resources, we should be able to get the best out of our relationships, complementing each other's strengths and accepting each other's limitations.

Couples

Most permanent relationships are happy to begin with. But things are rarely always harmonious and as your life and circumstances change, the strength of your relationship depends on your ability to adapt. You can hardly expect to know everything there is to know about your partner, or they about you, until events arise to test your resources as individuals and as a couple. What is more, there is no such thing as a "typical" couple. Everyone has their own weaknesses and strengths and your success as a team depends very much on your ability to recognize what these are and to adapt accordingly. Expecting your partner to live up to an unrealistic image that you have imposed on them puts a great strain on a relationship. Assuming that you or your partner will always be as good tempered, patient, unselfish, and calm as you perhaps were early on in the relationship is both unrealistic and unfair.

Human frailty and fallibility narrow our chances of finding the 100 per cent perfect partner or of filling that role ourselves. The sooner you can love unconditionally, accept your partner's failings, and concentrate on their good points, the more easily you will be able to resolve any problems. Shaping and nurturing a lifelong partnership requires a lot of self awareness and effort. Knowing how to give as well as take, being able to work out fair compromises when conflicts of interests, needs, and opinions arise will prevent you from developing feelings of self-blame, guilt, or resentment which could lead to the souring or break-up of a relationship.

The language of touch can be one of the most direct forms of communication between two people.

Conflicts and communication

There are conflicts in even the happiest relationships. You will be able to resolve them more easily if you cultivate communication skills. To do this, you must first establish a sound basis for communication. You should both be able to talk openly about individual concerns when they arise, before they turn into major issues. Develop a positive mind and the ability to stand back and see situations objectively before arguments begin. Talk things through calmly. Try to understand your partner's point of view, so that it is easier for you to reach a reasonable compromise.

It is not only what you say that affects how well you communicate. Your tone of voice, facial expression, movements, and gestures are non-verbal signals and clues that reveal your true feelings. Be alert and sensitive to these signals in your partner and express yourself clearly to encourage empathy. When problems appear to be insurmountable, remember that you do have a choice of actions and attitudes which will enable you to cope more successfully.

Preparing for the stress points

Pressures on a relationship can occur at any time, but there are particular transition phases and experiences that force us to revalue and adapt our role. You can predict many of these points and prepare yourself, so that when they arrive, they are not so stressful.

Falling in love, courting, dating, and getting to know one another usually make up a couple's most carefree period. The stresses associated with getting engaged and married, or starting to live together, are usually resolved quite easily. Often, they are prompted mainly by pressures from relatives or by small differences of opinion–something that is normal when two people are trying to mesh their individual lifestyles into one. As you settle down, finding out things that irritate or disappoint you about your partner may cause tensions. But these can be offset by the security of having a settled relationship. More major, potentially stressful events that face the majority of couples are buying a home and having children. The exhaustion and strain of house-hunting and moving are relatively short-lived, while the financial burden of paying off a mortgage tends to become less onerous as time goes on. Starting a family can involve a more complex series of stresses. Unplanned pregnancy or the inability to conceive may cause both partners deep and lasting trauma, involving decisions on emotional issues such as abortion, adoption, treatment for infertility, or artificial fertilization. Childbirth then brings with it the possible risk of post-natal depression, exhaustion, and a disrupted sex life. Coping with young children may prove physically tiring for both partners, especially if you go out to work. It also alters your way of life by limiting the

Coping with young children is tiring–but also very rewarding.

The later years can be the most fulfilling if you have close bonds of intimacy and trust.

opportunity to do things alone and the nature of the
activities you pursue.

Later on, adolescent problems can cause family friction and divided loyalties, while middle age heralds a
change in roles and lifestyle prompted by a number of
significant factors. As the children grow up and leave
home and the time for retirement approaches, your
own parents may become ill, grow more dependent, or
die, and women may be faced with unpleasant
psychological and physical symptoms of the
menopause. The interest and joy of having grandchild-
ren gives you a new role and can make up for any
regrets that your days of active parenting are over.
Other factors to which you may have to adjust are the
changes that occur when the pull and challenge of full-
time employment are replaced by leisure time, if physical strength and activity are impaired by ill health and
if your relationship relies increasingly on close com-
panionship rather than sexual passion and physical
attraction. The closer your bond of humour, intimacy,
and trust, the greater your chances of turning this into
one of the most fulfilling times of your life. Shared
interests and activities that continue into middle age
will also help make your later years enjoyable.

Sex and stress

Eroticism is one of the most pleasurable and natural of
human drives. A powerful and satisfying means of
human communication, good sex between a loving
couple is about giving and receiving both love and
physical pleasure. It should involve our spiritual and
emotional as well as our erotic and physical selves,
drawing us closer together. Sex is a form of communication that can be more eloquent than words. But we
must be able to talk about it if we are to enjoy a mutually satisfying relationship. When sex is a conversa-
tional taboo, it is difficult for you to make your sexual
needs clear to your partner. The result can be doubts,
inhibitions, and frustrations. So as early as possible,
try to be specific about what turns you on–or off–and
encourage your partner to do likewise. Use humour,
tact, and loving gentleness when broaching the subject
of sex and never bring it up when things get tense.

*Talking, loving support,
and understanding are
essential in a good couple
relationship.*

Try to understand how your partner's body works
and talk about the differences between the sexes. Men
should be aware of the way a woman's changing hor-
monal cycle affects her, how choice of contraception
can help or hinder a woman's responses, and how the
months following childbirth and the period of the
menopause may affect a woman's capacity for sexual
enjoyment. Women, on the other hand, should
become aware of how stress can cause premature eja-
culation or impotence in men. Talking, loving support,
and understanding can help with these problems.

If you cannot talk openly, use the body's physical
language. You will overcome embarrassment by being
more tactile and physically demonstrative. Hugging,
kissing, holding hands, stroking, and just holding each
other creates intimacy and removes inhibitions.

Normality and you

Explicit media coverage of sex can lead us to believe
that some things are normal and accepted while others
are not. This can spark feelings of inadequacy about
our sexual habits and preferences. But normality is not
important when it comes to sex. What matters is
whether what you do and how you do it pleases you
and your partner, not whether other people do it.
Needs vary tremendously from couple to couple, individual to individual. But you should be able to compromise if your needs as individuals vary greatly.

Good sex does not always come spontaneously. If
you lead a busy, stressful life, you may need to plan
ahead the best times to enjoy sex. This isn't coldly cal-
culating, it is an intensely personal matter, involving
candid discussion with your partner.

If you have a serious sexual problem, try consulting a
sex counsellor about your fears. We can all learn and
perfect new techniques and expand our capacity for enjoyment. This is something that comes not only
through sexual expertise but also as a result of increased confidence. Discovering your own sexuality
and developing preferences takes time as well as practise. Your sexual capacity and expertise will develop as
much as a result of self knowledge as through experi-
menting sexually with your partner.

*The physical language of
the body also gives you a
way of helping you relax
on your own. Soothe away
tensions with firm, even
strokes.*

Families and groups

Confidence is contagious. If you are happy and confident about your own qualities, you are likely to have a harmonious family life. It also helps to be assertive about your needs–respect and regard from your family will be more naturally and freely forthcoming. A sense of humour, consideration for others, and respect for the changing needs of your family are other qualities that are best taught by example. Don't set yourself impossibly high standards of perfection as a wife, housekeeper, or parent in a bid to "earn" love or be worthy of the respect of your family. Allow yourself to be loved, as you undoubtedly are, for yourself as a person, complete with your qualities and faults. Accept and like who you are, be open about your likes, needs, and emotions, and you will encourage an open, honest, and understanding family atmosphere built on good communication. In a similar way, it is unfair to make unreasonable demands or harbour high expectations of your children. There is no reason why they should share your interests and fulfil your ambitions. Allow them instead the freedom to develop as individuals. This in turn provides a nurturing environment in which they can develop and have room to grow and express themselves freely and honestly.

Giving, taking, and sharing

Families need discipline as well as love. A framework of rules, administered in a caring way, prevents domestic chaos and creates a more harmonious, balanced daily life. Bringing up very young children to observe discipline and learn the rudiments of good behaviour and manners establishes respect for you as parents and makes later conflict less likely. As they get older, consult your children about issues that affect the family as a whole. Talk together as a family about education, sex, health, nutrition, leisure, and finance. Considering their needs and wishes and involving them in discussion teaches them to observe your needs and encourages mutual respect. In addition, they will develop their own resources and decision-making ability, becoming more willing and able to take up family responsibilities and to make decisions for themselves.

   You should extend this co-operation to day-to-day

Like two musicians playing together, any group of people needs communication and mutual understanding to develop a successful relationship.

tasks. Ask all family members to take equal turns to prepare meals, go shopping, do housework and be responsible for doing their own laundry. If you are a working mother, avoid the "superwoman syndrome" of fitting in all the cooking and housework single-handed before and after work. Sons who observe—and help—their father doing their fair share of domestic tasks will become more self sufficient and are less likely to dismiss this as a woman's responsibility when they grow up. Try to swap and share roles with your partner whenever you can. Aim to be a *friend* to your children, so that you all collaborate as a close-knit family team.

Money

Many people find that money is a major stress in their lives. This is not necessarily because they don't have enough of it. The root of the problem is that people do not discuss money enough. Consequently, children often grow up ignorant about the financial side of running a home, buying or renting real estate, living independently, and balancing income and expenditure. Reluctance to talk openly about money often stems from unpleasant memories of a childhood beset by financial worries or poverty. Also, because of society's values we often tend to measure self-esteem in relation to our earning power. So a badly paid job can diminish self-esteem and self-confidence, making it more difficult and embarrassing to discuss finances openly with other people.

By sitting down with your children and explaining the basic principles of money management they will more readily adopt a reasonable attitude toward money—yours as well as theirs. In addition, this financial knowledge will be of inestimable value to your children when they grow up. Helping them work out electricity and gas rates, understand telephone charges, guiding them through insurance policies, and explaining how tax is assessed, equips them to become responsible adults and ensures they are less likely to drift into financial difficulties when they leave home. Try to demonstrate by example as well as through practical instruction how and where to save money effectively.

BUDGETING	
Weekly Travel Food	**Quarterly** Electricity Gas Telephone
Monthly Rent/mortgage Rates Credit cards	**Annual** Insurance Water rates Vacation Christmas

Much financial stress comes from lack of planning. Make a list of regular outgoings, writing the amounts you expect to spend next to each item. You will then know how much money you are likely to have left. This is also useful as a method of teaching children about budgeting.

Groups outside the family

Being self-sufficient as a family unit encourages close-ness but if we want to broaden our interests and develop friendships we must find ways of establishing other relationships with colleagues and friends outside the family. Getting to know and forming friendships with people from different countries, walks of life and backgrounds ultimately teaches us much about ourselves as well as about humanity and the nature and problems of society. Our need for close, loving friendships increases as we get older and may complement or provide a substitute for family relationships at times of trouble and stress. Follow your instincts in picking friends, and nurture your friendships. They need almost as much give and take, compromise and commitment, as family relationships. Try sometimes to overlook age barriers when forming friendships. An older mentor or confidante can offer understanding, wisdom, and impartial advice in difficult situations when parental communication is limited or if you have no immediate family to consult.

Support groups

When you have a problem it is often better to talk to someone outside your immediate circle of family and friends. The closer you are to someone, the harder it is for them to offer advice since they know you too well and tend to be emotionally involved. Apart from this, they may lack the sort of professional expertise needed to provide answers to your questions. Generally speaking you should consult a good doctor for any health problems and a gynaecologist or family planning clinic for anything connected with contraception, conception, and sexually transmitted diseases. Sex therapists and counsellors who specialize in family and emotional problems deal with a wide variety of personal and relationship problems, while the citizen's advice bureau or a lawyer or accountant can advise on matters relating to finance, divorce, and the law in general. Drug addiction, alcoholism, depression, loneliness, and rape, are just some of the crises that have recently spawned their own support groups or advice centres where you can go for practical help.

An older mentor or confidante can offer understanding and wisdom.

The art of working

Work dominates our lives. Most people work eight hours a day. Add to this the time spent travelling to and from work, preparing and cleaning up, and overtime, and the total is often far greater. Work and work-related activities account for the major part of our waking hours for five or six days a week.

Western society is founded on the work ethic. This tends to make our attitude to work stoical and serious. We put in long hours, and we often silently suffer uncomfortable working conditions. We also tend to seek promotion as an emblem of success rather than a means of fulfilment, and to link our self-esteem with our earning power. Happiness still comes somewhat low on most peoples' lists of work priorities, but work-related stress is increasingly recognized today as a major cause of illness and mental breakdown.

Fortunately, our view of work is starting to change. Our demands and expectations are centred not only on pay and working conditions but now also take into account the quality of work and job satisfaction. Working also gives us a sense of belonging and purpose. In a society built on commerce and industry, the work we do defines our role, strengthening our sense of identity and conferring responsibility.

In ideal circumstances our work can broaden the scope of our lives. When satisfaction and fulfilment are high, when we enjoy the job we do and do it well, the challenges and opportunities afforded by giving of our best can encourage us to grow and develop as human beings. Recognition of our talents is therefore central to job satisfaction. The other ingredients of job satisfaction depend on the individual. For some people, security is the most important element, for others, it is the freedom to set their own targets.

Faced with increased work stress (and the phenomenon of "burnout" at all levels of the workforce), more and more employers are beginning to restructure their working methods, rethink company policy and improve communications and relations between management and workers. One solution is to give employees more control, which helps to avoid feelings of frustration.

Too little work, and the boredom and frustration resulting from unemployment, also cause stress. The best solution here is to learn self-discipline to prevent the drift into purposelessness.

But the structure of employment and the way we work is beginning to change. Redundancy, unemployment, and shorter working days are increasingly common, and have their benefits as well as their drawbacks. More emphasis on leisure time and improved quality of life is causing us to revalue both our job expectations and our style of working. A shorter working day, automation, flexitime, job sharing, and the use of computer links offer a range of new working styles. They also indicate a new and welcome humanization of the overall concept of work. A freer, more open system of communication and improved working relations lead us inevitably toward greater say and control over how our working lives are run. These are essential changes to strive for if we are to experience less stress and enjoy happier, more harmonious working lives.

Organizing your work

Plan your work and you will immediately feel less stressed about it. Lack of proper organization and planning is probably the most common basic cause of self-generated stress at work. Imposing a structure on your working day and carrying out tasks and duties according to a distinct pattern makes you feel more in control. The pattern should not be rigid–a certain amount of variety is also essential. But only you know your capabilities and can gauge the right balance to strike between routine and flexibility. There are many ways you can organize your work more efficiently. Making lists and timetables, keeping a diary, and working out priorities all help to avoid chaos and confusion. They will allow you to keep control of what you do by matching your style and rhythm of working to the demands of the job. Thinking problems through logically, writing down the various solutions, and using logic diagrams will also help you organize your work and plan your activities.

Routine and variety
Too much routine dulls your mind and saps your energies. But being faced with a multiplicity of tasks and responsibilities can lead to disorganization and muddle. Too much of either in the end is stressful, so you should strike the right balance between the two states to maintain efficiency and enjoyment in your work. If yours is a hectic job with more than its fair share of variety and the unexpected, working to a timetable that allows you to clear routine jobs and mail at a regular time will help to impose more order in your life and work. You should also learn to say "no" when you are asked to do too many things at once and be ready to delegate work to others when your schedule is full. If you have a job dominated by routine, learn how to interrupt monotony by planning ahead. Work out when you can stop doing certain tasks and switch to others, or when you can take periods off to relax. Learn how to stop, stand back, and get some satisfaction from your work. Even if you are very busy, occasional periods of relaxation will pay dividends, both in making you feel better, and in increased efficiency when you start working again.

Like juggling, the challenge of organizing is to keep everything moving in a smooth, continuous rhythm.

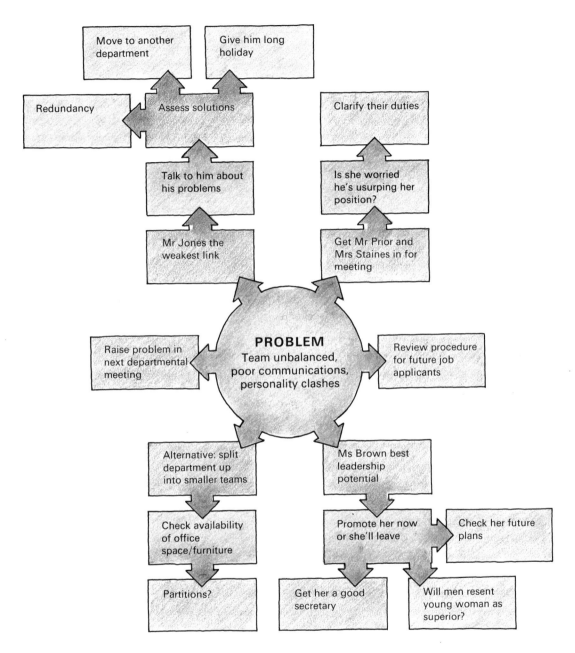

Move to another department

Give him long holiday

Redundancy

Assess solutions

Clarify their duties

Talk to him about his problems

Is she worried he's usurping her position?

Mr Jones the weakest link

Get Mr Prior and Mrs Staines in for meeting

Raise problem in next departmental meeting

PROBLEM
Team unbalanced, poor communications, personality clashes

Review procedure for future job applicants

Alternative: split department up into smaller teams

Ms Brown best leadership potential

Check availability of office space/furniture

Promote her now or she'll leave

Check her future plans

Partitions?

Get her a good secretary

Will men resent young woman as superior?

Organizational skills

Keeping diaries, schedules, and lists will obviously help you to organize your work. But if you have a difficult problem to solve, you may find that a simple list will not help very much. If this happens, try making a logic diagram, writing the basic problem in the middle, and grouping related thoughts, questions, and possible solutions on branches radiating outward. This type of diagram grows organically according to the particular problem and quickly shows you how its various elements relate to each other.

Job satisfaction

The happier and more satisfied you are in your job the less likely you are to suffer from stress. Many different things influence job satisfaction. The principle factors are: the degree of control you have over the way you do your job, the scope you have for pride in the work you do, the amount of recognition you receive, the environment you work in, the person you work for, security, money, and promotion prospects. Some of these influences are beyond our control. But a change in attitude can often yield surprising benenfits. Learn to be self-motivated. This will help you recognize and take pride in your own worth and abilities. You can also increase your level of satisfaction by setting your own short- and long-term goals. This will add interest and purpose to your work if feedback from your colleagues or boss is limited. Finally, don't get trapped in a treadmill. Whenever you can, find the time to stand back from your work and take some pride and enjoyment in a job well done. You will work more efficiently after a short break.

Social organization

People matter more than anything else when it comes to happiness at work. It is not only the individuals we work with, but the way they are grouped together that is important. Most people work best in small teams. Personality, team spirit, plus your own need for privacy or for other people determine the size of the team in which you will work at your best. This is an element over which we have little or no control, so try to remain adaptable. Teams of four to eight people work well and split up easily into smaller groups. The smaller the group, the better its members need to get on with one another to avoid creating an atmosphere of friction and tension, something you must bear in mind when applying for or entering a new job. Crowding can be highly stressful and as isolating as true isolation. The actual size of your work area is almost as important as the number of people, since it determines your physical proximity to others and sets the boundaries of personal territory. Open-plan work spaces limit privacy and are noisier but they encourage access and communication.

Craftspeople often have more scope for job satisfaction than those in other occupations. They have the advantage of being able to stand back and admire a finished object that they have created.

The working environment

Like any other environment, the workplace can contribute to our well-being or militate against our mood. Faced with drab, impersonal, uncomfortable, and overcrowded work areas, our sense of impotence and frustration can be overwhelming. But there are small, subtle ways in which you can improve a depressing, ugly work environment. Brighten and cheer up your section of wall with posters, pictures, cards, and plants. Bring in fresh flowers and use as many things as you can that appeal to your own personal taste.

The more potential dangers there are in your work place, the more aware of safety procedures you have to be. If you work in a factory, make sure that you always use your equipment and machinery according to the instructions. Avoid time-saving short cuts if they are likely to jeopardize safety. Ensure that everyone is aware of safety regulations. Even offices have their hazards. Avoid trailing electrical flexes and poorly balanced filing cabinets that might tip over.

Combatting pollution at work

Proper ventilation is vital. It can counteract the effects of overcrowding, cigarette smoke, the build-up of static electricity, dust, and vapour emitted by chemical substances. Natural ventilation is more efficient and better for you than air conditioning. This in itself can become a source of "office sickness" with symptoms such as sinus congestion, itchy eyes, dry throat, headaches, and fatigue. Open the windows as often as possible especially if you work in a confined space with chemical materials. If you cannot escape air conditioning, keep the temperature at about 68°F (20°C), with a comfortable level of humidity. Plants, flowers, and bowls of water will increase the humidity. Air ionizers counteract stuffiness and drowsiness, catarrh, and eye problems, by keeping the air fresh and charged with negative ions. A strict no-smoking rule will also help keep the atmosphere clear.

Use VDUs with care. Ration time spent using them, control the brightness, and keep them serviced. Keep copying machines in a room separate from the main workspace. Cut out static with chemicals and mats, and improve the lighting with full-spectrum bulbs.

Ionizers help combat stuffiness, while plants have a beneficial influence on the humidity.

Talking

Whatever your work, communication is a vital skill. If you are timid and unassertive you will be frustrated at not being noticed or understood. But if you are too aggressive, people will ignore you too. Either way, you will feel resentful. Before this happens, enlist the help of a colleague if there is a problem involving your team or department. Plan a course of action and write down the salient points you want to raise. If you are not on relaxed or friendly terms with your superior but need to set up a meeting, try to gain the confidence of his or her secretary or next-in-command and establish the best time and method of approach. If you feel you have prepared well, you will be more confident.

In any discussion, don't be on the offensive. You are out to talk, not to do battle. A relaxed, smiling, non-aggressive attitude keeps a civilized discussion from turning into a confrontation. Do not interrupt other people or finish their sentences for them. Let them finish speaking, then speak, resisting interruption in turn. Never raise your voice or use threatening movements or postures and try not to become emotional. Your views have a better chance of being considered if you put them over with a balance of logic, assertiveness, and good humour.

Solving communications problems

Many factors can impair communications at work. A hierarchical structure can cause barriers. For example, if there is an autocratic, decision-making boss at the top, and employees with no say in work policy below, there may be little chance to communicate freely. It is usually the style of management that dictates the style of communications at work. An employer who manages by putting people first and encouraging participation in decision-making will foster team spirit and communications between departments. Inflexibility of manner and attitude, on the other hand, narrow the channels of communication.

When conflicts do arise, act promptly. Postponing action makes things worse, making it harder to broach the subject. Approaching a problem obliquely, using tactical skills to affect a solution, may be necessary if communication channels are limited.

Gestures can help or hinder communication. An open, supplicatory gesture (top) is welcoming and suggests that you can listen as well as talk. But pushing the palms away from you (centre) or making chopping gestures (above) can repel or distract the listener.

Meeting challenges

Most of us seek a balance of being able to do our jobs easily and efficiently on a day-to-day basis while rising to extra demands if they are made. We get a feeling of security from the day-to-day work, while the challenges generate intellectual or creative stimulus.

This balance is often difficult to achieve. Jobs involving constant deadlines and responsibilites can leave you feeling overstressed, unable to cope, or exhausted. This often happens after a promotion. Control excessive demands by learning when to say no or when to take a break. Doing extra preparatory work and being better organized also helps. Don't rush, do one thing at a time, and do the difficult jobs first.

If you prefer to work at a slower pace, choose a job of greater predictability with just the occasional extra demand. But remember that boredom and frustration can be as stressful as an overdemanding job. Short of changing jobs, becoming self-motivated or seeking promotion or extra responsibilities are the only ways of trying to stretch yourself. Stress may also be caused by frustration at having insufficient authority and control in your job or too few responsibilities.

Problems at work
You will find solutions to some other work problems in Chapter 15 (see pp. 172-87).

TASKS AT WORK

Type of work	What's needed	Typical tasks
Organizational	Quick thinking, knowing own schedule, access to others	Anything involving other people's schedules; making appointments, drawing up schedules; arranging conferences; delegating; writing memos
Physical	Energy and time	General physical work; clearing up; travelling
Creative	Mental clarity, ability to concentrate	Using imagination and manual dexterity; designing and drawing; writing; craft work; planning sales demonstrations or PR work
Mundane	Perseverance, regular application	Simple repetitive work; answering routine letters; making phone calls; dealing with queries; doing simple accounts
Research and preparatory work	Concentration, quiet environment, no interruptions	Library and archive work; reading; making lists; drawing up plans and charts; laboratory work; buying raw materials; mending and renewing equipment
Communication	Planning, confidence, correct timing, alertness	Asking for a pay rise or promotion; dealing with complaints; having to dismiss or demote a colleague or employee; conducting interviews; participating in a conference, seminar, or meeting.

PROBLEM-SOLVING		
Problem	**Immediate solution**	**Long-term solution**
You want a pay increase, promotion, extra holiday	Send a memo to see employer, or make direct request.	If request is denied, propose again later; write a letter stating your case; threaten to resign; look for a job with better conditions.
Alienation, lack of participation in policy; you feel cut off, ignorant of the work of the organization as a whole and of how decisions are made	Enlist the help of co-workers; talk with counterparts in other parts of the organization to learn more about their work; talk with workers in similar organizations to exchange views.	Encourage more team spirit within departments; set up monthly meetings to cover progress and policy making; suggest that management also join in to encourage greater participation in decision making, free flow of communications up, down, and across company structure.
You want a safer, cleaner, more comfortable work environment or equipment	Check with union or colleagues that request is reasonable; send a memo making your request; if nothing is forthcoming, try to improve conditions yourself; bring in your own replacement; rearrange equipment or furniture; clean up your workspace.	File a formal complaint to your employer; if employer will not give you your rights, threaten to take legal action.
Your immediate superior is rude, dismissive, or will not listen to your request	Avoid becoming emotional; learn to be assertive without being aggressive; stay as pleasant as possible; remember it's their problem, not yours; try to be aware of the factors in the other person's life that might be causing their problems and attitudes.	Write a letter of complaint to the person concerned or their superior; confront the person with your complaints over a meeting after work; if things get too stressful, resign; ensure that your employer knows the reasons.
Your boss has a way of creating last-minute pressures and extra demands; you like the challenge and feel flattered, but are getting stressed in spite of good organization	Say "no" sometimes, when appropriate, and explain why; tell your boss that you will deal with extra work in your own time or will delegate; if you are on friendly terms, have a chat over drinks or lunch and discuss your future.	Work out a more structured schedule that allows for extra demands; delegate or share responsibilities; ask for promotion, salary increase, or assistance; give up the job if the stress is becoming an unavoidable element that you don't enjoy.

Analysing your work

To sort out the various tasks and challenges involved in your job, make a list (opposite) of the types of work that you do. This may be useful in helping you to plan more variety in your working day. It may also help you organize better: you can group together the various tasks that are best done at the same time. You can use the same sort of list to work out the type of work you are good at–useful when looking for a job. An analytical approach will also be helpful when you are trying to deal with problems at work (above). Here, it is useful to divide the solutions into short- and long-term, so that you can plan your strategy. The chart on this page gives a range of suggestions for some of the most common work problems.

Planning your time

From the revolution of the planets around the sun to our own biological clock, our entire universe is ruled by rhythm. Punctuated by sunrise and sunset, light and darkness, our daily, or "circadian", cycle dominates our lives. It regulates our periods of sleep, hunger, and activity by controlling mood, mental alertness, and bodily functions. The way the body clock is set varies from person to person. This fact explains why some people operate at their best early in the day, others late at night.

Whatever we are doing, time is a precious commodity. There are only 24 hours in each day, and for most of us these are divided up into day-time working hours and night-time rest. Fitting in all your tasks, commitments, and leisure activities into your waking hours can create time shortages. The longer and more demanding your work schedule and home life, the greater the risk of becoming a victim of what stress researchers call "hurry sickness". Those most likely to suffer are highly stressed type-A personalities, for whom the stress of time-urgency tends to be self-generated. Worried that there never seems to be enough time to get anything done, type-A people often leave insufficient time to complete tasks, try to cram too many activities into a short period, or do several things at once, darting haphazardly from one to another. The immediate consequences of this type of behaviour are familiar: undone jobs pile up or are completed late, deadlines loom, tempers are lost, and anxiety and panic ensue.

Work is not the only thing that suffers when this happens. Relationships and home life become subject to the same panic pressures and time shortages. Resentment at too much time spent working, too little relaxing and enjoying the company of family and friends, is bound to limit the amount of satisfaction you derive from life in general. But if you have too much time to spare, as a result of unemployment or underwork, you are also likely to have problems. The lack of mental and physical stimulus can lead to feelings of depression and isolation.

To avoid these traps you must be able to control your relationship to time. The most effective way of doing this involves very careful planning: assessing your capabilities and working out schedules. This chapter shows you the organizational strategies you can use to do this. The result should be that you will be able to get more done in the hours available to you, with a better balance of work, home, and leisure activities.

One of the most important points to remember is that you should schedule your leisure activities as carefully as your work. This will help you realize how important leisure and relaxation are to your overall health and well-being.

Scheduling your actitivtes will prevent work from impinging on home life, a prime source of domestic tension that can build up gradually and unknowingly. Our working and home lives are, after all, closely interdependent and, under ideal circumstances, they should complement and enhance one another. So the great advantage of balancing work and leisure is that it enhances the quality of both, helping you to feel good and to give of your best.

Analysing time

Few of us have complete control over our time. The way you divide up your hours inevitably depends on the nature of your work and the structure of your personal life. The ideal balance of roughly eight hours spent at work and the rest of the time relaxing and enjoying yourself is hard for most people to achieve all the time. Under pressure you may lose sight of priorities, allowing certain areas and activities to crowd out the others, with the result that life can become increasingly stressful or monotonous, devoid of stimulus or fun. Sleeping and eating are obviously vital functions to which we must devote sufficient time. But it is also important to learn to how to waste time creatively. Indulging periodically in some apparently aimless or indolent pastime can prove therapeutic, because it increases your efficiency and contentment at work, as well as your capacity to unwind. Giving yourself a break to laze, day-dream, or play, calms your body and mind, recharges your energy, and inspires optimism, contentment, and humour.

Too many hours spent working, together with an average amount of sleep, is not enough to create a balance of time. You also need time to relax.

Balancing time – home and work

Do not spend too much time on any one activity. You cannot hope to devote most of your waking hours to your job without affecting the quality of other areas of your life. Hard work over long periods leads to tension and tiredness, which in turn limits your ability to relax and enjoy leisure. So the busier your work schedule, the more important it is to take time off regularly. Exercising, meditating, listening to music, reading, cooking, and socializing are just some activities which redress the balance of a demanding work schedule. Plan your leisure activities and create time to relax. If you have too much time, take up a new hobby or sport, or do voluntary work.

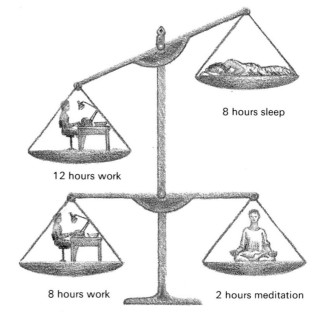

8 hours sleep

12 hours work

8 hours work

2 hours meditation

Allowing time for travel, a normal eight-hour working day should leave you with at least two full *hours to spend relaxing, exercising, or meditating. With sleep, this will give a balance of time.*

Balancing time – self and others

A happy home and family environment should offer the most harmonious contrast to your working life and to the stresses of travelling to and from work. But the family can also place demands on you that may prove stressful. The larger your family, and the more extensive your group activities with the children, the less opportunity you may find to spend time with your partner. And the more time you spend with other people, the more important it is to keep some time to spend on your own. Creating time for you and your partner to relax, resolve problems, and share one another's daily experiences is essential. Too little time together may cause unnecessary conflicts and misunderstandings. Put aside private times to be alone with your partner. And don't feel guilty about taking time to be alone. Privacy is a very real need, not a luxury. Time to yourself, perhaps exercising, reading, or listening to music, gives you space and quietness to relax, to sort out your thoughts, and to gain perspective on issues both at work and at home.

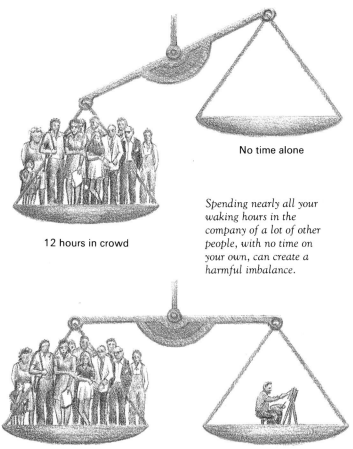

No time alone

12 hours in crowd

Spending nearly all your waking hours in the company of a lot of other people, with no time on your own, can create a harmful imbalance.

2 hours in crowd   **2 hours on your own**

To get the right balance of time with others and on your own, spend an hour alone for every hour spent in a crowd or with several other people.

4 hours with family   **2 hours on your own**

Offset family time by spending a few minutes on your own at regular intervals through the day.

Organizing time

Organize your time efficiently and you will feel you are in control of your life. You should allocate precise and appropriate times for activities and set priorities for the tasks you need to complete. If you do this, you will balance and match your demands with your supply of available time and stop channelling too many activities into a limited or narrow time-span. This will allow you to pace yourself correctly, giving you room for error, instead of letting you be taken unawares by unexpected time pressures. The further ahead you can plan your timetable the better. You should plan on several different levels, to give varying perspectives on how you need to spend your time. Use a 6 or 12 month long-term schedule in conjunction with an interim monthly listing; sub-divide the month into detailed short-term weekly schedules; and make daily lists of what you have to do. When an unexpected problem arises, don't panic–work out how much time it will take to solve and insert it into your list.

Long-term planner
Using a six-monthly or yearly chart, mark down as precisely as possible your major work projects, meetings, and estimated work load, including shift work, overtime, and anything else connected with work that is likely to demand extra time. Note social and family occasions, holidays, and times when you must give priority to family matters.

HALF-YEARLY SCHEDULE

Month	Work	Family	Self
January	Clients from abroad at end of month – organize sales meetings	Plan summer vacation	
February	Colleague on holiday – extra work – ask for help early in month	Make dental appointments	Arrange to meet visitors from overseas
March	New client at end of month	Parents' wedding anniversary – arrange celebration	Renew insurance policies
April	Accounts for end of financial year – get extra help	Easter 2 weeks' vacation for children	
May			Long weekend – golf tournament – book hotel in advance
June	New boss at start of month – more work at transfer period	School exams	

MONTHLY SCHEDULE

Day	Week 1	Week 2	Week 3	Week 4
Monday	Swimming Interview	Running Work at home in morning		Easter
Tuesday	Early meeting; lunch-time squash	Swimming Work at home in morning	Running	Day off
Wednesday	Work late	Running Work at home in morning	Trip to conference	Redecorate kitchen
Thursday	Running	Swimming Concert at school	Running Parents' wedding anniversary	Redecorate kitchen
Friday	Swimming Finish work early Pack for weekend	Running	Swimming Easter	Running Birthday
Weekend	Staying with friends	Work Sat.	Easter	

Monthly listings
On a monthly list (above), enter the same information as on your long-term planner, but in greater detail, as your schedule becomes more definite.

Weekly diary
On this list everything you have to do in order of priority (right). Write each item into the appropriate day and block of time allocated. Estimate how much time you need to complete each task, and add to this 10 or 20 per cent to allow for errors or problems.

WEEKLY DIARY

Monday
7.00 am Yoga
8.30 am Meet colleague at airport
3.30 pm Arrange to meet new staff member
7.30 pm Birthday dinner

Tuesday
7.00 am Yoga
9–11.00 am Work on project for tomorrow's meeting
3.00 pm Meeting with boss
4.30 pm Leave work early – take children to barbeque

Wednesday
7.00 am Yoga
9.30 am Planning meeting for new long-term projects
1.00 pm Lunch with new client
5.50 pm Go swimming

Thursday
7.00 am Yoga
1.00 pm Do shopping for this evening's meal
3–5.00 pm Appointments
6–7.00 pm Cook meal
8.30 pm Dinner with friends

Friday
7.00 am Yoga
1.00 pm Work through lunch to prepare for next week's conference
4.30 pm Look through next week's diary
7.30 pm Movies

Saturday/Sunday
Saturday Shopping
Sunday Day in the country with family

De-stressed schedules

Your job and home life dictate how much flexibility and control you have over your schedules. Many types of work involve very rigid schedules with little freedom to change working hours. In addition, everyone tends to begin and end their working day at the same time, which means that there is a danger of boredom, crowding, and discomfort during rush-hours. These factors can cause a feeling that you are a prisoner of time. But you can at least plan ahead your recreational and domestic activities to add variety to evenings, weekends, and holidays, and make up for the rigid working week. You can avoid rigidity if you have a certain freedom about when you begin and finish work. If this is the case, you can set off for work and return home earlier or later than the main rush. If you can choose where you live and work, you can avoid the crush by travelling in the opposite direction to the majority. In most cities, the prevailing direction is toward the centre in the morning, away from the centre at night. Working from home in theory offers the ultimate freedom of choice, though some people find it monotonous, and self-discipline is essential.

Flexible work schedule

Variable work hours allow you the greatest freedom to divide up your working and leisure time. Being self-employed, freelance, or doing a part-time job, means you can stagger your workload. You can leave for work a little earlier or later in the day to miss the rush hour, or stay on later to avoid the evening rush. Flexible lunch breaks provide an extra opportunity for relaxation periods, while combining an office schedule with periods of working from home gives you more opportunity to spend time with your family.

FLEXI-TIME WORKER		
7.30 am Read paper; dictate letters on dictaphone		**1.30 pm** Late lunch: ¼ hour meditation; ¾ hour meal
8.00 am Exercise for ½ hour before breakfast		**4.30 pm** Relax: 10 minute tea-break; assess work done
9.00 am Leave work; avoid rush hour		**7.00 pm** Spend two hours with family; dinner
10.00 am Priority phone calls		**9.00 pm** Plan work for next day
12.00 am Work on special project		**10.30 pm** Relax; chat with partner before bed

The parent at home

Every parent looking after babies or young children all day is familiar with occasional feelings of loneliness and boredom. Over a long period, endless household chores, the lack of mental stimulus, and the absence of social contact may lead to discontentment and depression. But you can plan your day to shop and travel at the most convenient times. Try to enlist the help of family and friends if you need a break from child-minding and housework. Socialize with other parents and build a supporting network. Sharing out the responsibility for minding the children provides you with the opportunity to leave the home environment, take some exercise, and do something you really want to do.

PARENT	
7.00 am Breakfast	2.00 pm Parents' get-together; take baby to park
7.30 am Drive partner to station	3.00 pm Prepare dinner for evening
8.30 am Take children to school	3.30 pm Yoga or meditation
9.30 am Do shopping	4.00 pm Collect children from school
11.00 am Tea break with friend	5.00 pm Help children with homework
12.00 am Housework while listening to music	8.00 pm Dinner
1.00 pm Sit down to lunch	9.00 pm Relax with partner

Working at home

This pattern of working provides the ideal opportunity to create your own work and leisure periods. But self-discipline is essential if you are to work efficiently, and you need the support of a family who respect your privacy during working hours. The boundaries between work and leisure can become blurred if you work from home, so to make sure you give adequate time and concentration to both, follow a strict schedule, as you would if you were working from an office.

HOME WORKER	
6.30 am Start work before family gets up	1.00 pm Lunch
8.00 am Breakfast with family	2.00 pm Work
9.00 am Exercise for 1 hour	6.00 pm Finish work; spend time with family
10.30 am Telephone calls	8.00 pm Dinner
11.00 am Work with friend; exercise	9.00 pm Relax with partner

Personal space and comfort

Our environment is an extension of ourselves. We adapt our "immediate surroundings" to suit our individual needs and comforts, so that our homes offer us the opportunity to be truly ourselves. Fashioning our environment according to preferences of colour, style, and dimensions, is a method of self-expression, a personal statement directly related to our sense of identity and a reflection of our emotional security and sense of belonging. Since environment and mood are closely linked, our surroundings, if they are to be truly relaxing and nurturing, should be as stress-free as possible. The ideal stressproofed home is one that shows a balanced choice of personal style and mood, sound and stillness, and a harmonious synthesis of different colours, light, and shade.

The quality and comfort of any home can be undermined in various ways. Some of the causes are easy to recognize and deal with. Removing unpleasant smells, controlling extremes of temperature, and coping with dirt and untidiness are part of the everyday business of running a home. To do this efficiently, carry out all your housekeeping work routinely and methodically on a rota basis, making sure you store and return things to their proper place so that you know where to find them. Clutter and disorganization can create mental stress, and lead to worry, anger and time wasted when you search for lost and misplaced possessions. Tidying up as you go along (for example, during cooking or when changing your clothes) prevents clutter

from building up in the first place. If you are untidy, clear up at least two or three times a week.

Broad or environmental stresses, such as noise and bad light, can be more insidious and less easy to control. Noise is a subtle stress factor and its effect is cumulative. It can lead to loss of concentration, irritability, and insomnia. It can also cause headaches and muscular tension. If noise is a problem, start by reducing the levels that you can control yourself. To cut out external noise try wax earplugs. Double glazing is an effective way of cutting out street noise.

Light is another influence over how relaxed we are. Most of us feel happier, healthier, and more energetic in bright, sunny weather. When we are constantly surrounded by artificial light we tend to feel tired and depressed. This is not simply a psychological effect. Scientists have recently discovered a link between natural daylight and hormone levels, emotional well-being, and reproductivity. Installing specially designed lights that mimic natural full-spectrum light can help to reduce seasonal depression and to improve concentration and energy.

There are many other ways of shaping your environment. Use time, ingenuity, and above all imagination to create areas of private space, and adapt your home to your body's needs and habits. Trust your instincts in choosing colour schemes, background fragrances, houseplants, and music. These are a few of the ways in which you can style, enrich, and stressproof your personal surroundings.

Personal space

Everyone needs a space they can call their own. With
some people this does not seem to be true. They can
concentrate in a crowd and seem calm surrounded by
chaos. But in fact they carry their own personal space
around with them, as a snail carries a shell. If you are
not this sort of person, you should set aside at least
one area as your private territory. You should do this
no matter how cramped your living accommodation or
how many people you share it with. Equally, everyone
else in the household should have their own space, so
you should respect the private areas of others. Your
personal space can be small and its boundaries need
not be extensive. But the space should be clearly identified as yours. If you work at home you will probably
need a complete room to yourself. You can use it as a
workshop, studio, or office and keep everything there
that you need for your work—equipment, files, books,
and telephone. Privacy and quiet are essential if you
conduct a lot of your business over the phone or work
with people. The alternative, if space is limited, is to
screen off a section of a part of your sitting room or
bedroom for your work. Smaller areas, where you can
spend time meditating, exercising or studying, are
easier to establish through ingenious and imaginative
use of interior design.

*Like a snail with its shell,
some people seem to carry
their personal space with
them at all times.*

Adapting space

Even the most limited interior can accommodate a
small personal area. Decide on the amount of room
available, then work out the best way of defining the
space. You should aim for adaptability and
efficiency—you do not necessarily need to build a new
wall in order to divide up a room. Clever use of blinds
and screens or free-standing shelves allows you to section off an area temporarily, providing what amounts
to an extra room. Venetian, cane, paper, or roller
blinds divide space temporarily, providing varying
degrees of opacity or a solid "wall" of colour. You can
pull blinds or curtains across from wall to wall or arrange large plants as leafy markers to set your space
apart from the rest of the room. Folding screens also
make attractive and adaptable room dividers. Attractive screens are available in a variety of different

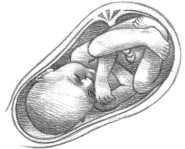

*The concept of personal
space is with us from the
beginning—even before
birth.*

materials–wood, lacquer, bamboo, or fabric-covered–and you can adjust them to divide off your work or study area, then fold them away or use them elsewhere in the home.

There does not have to be a physical division. Rugs placed on wall or floor, pictures, and mirrors, create clear patches of colour and texture in contrast to the overall surroundings, defining your space more subtly. You can also use spotlights in this way, strategically focusing pools of light on your table or desk and highlighting and identifying a small area to set it apart from the overall surrounding space. Keep your possessions in your personal space. For storage use decorative boxes, chests, or giant wicker baskets to eliminate clutter and emphasize privacy. More adaptable multi-tiered storage units are useful for work equipment. Some are available in the form of mobile trolleys. Another way of adapting a space to different functions is to use a sofa-bed or a bed that folds back flat into the wall by day. This means that you can convert a day-time work-room or sitting room into a bedroom, making economical use of a small space.

Architectural space

If the architecture of your home allows it, you can make more radical changes and create extra spaces within an existing interior. But before you begin to re-organize your home, try to eliminate clutter. Limit your storage areas to cellar, loft, attic, cupboards, and chests. If you have a room used only for storage, convert it into your own personal space–where you can work, read, or exercise. A room can fulfil more than one function.

If your ceilings are 13 ft (4 m) or higher, you can split the space horizontally by building a gallery to provide an extra elevated area. This could become a study, dining room, or sitting area. It is possible to damp-proof an unused cellar, install a ventilating system and turn it into an extra room. Bay windows and alcoves can become restful, cushioned seating areas for reading and relaxing. An alcove has the added advantage that you can screen it off temporarily when you need extra privacy or a temporary storage area.

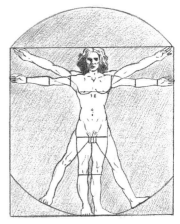

Proportion and balance are fundamental to humanity–something that it is important to remember when you are planning any personal space.

Creating comfort

Comfort depends on a whole range of complementary influences. As well as obvious things, such as the design of beds and chairs, there are "hidden" comfort factors, of which we may not be aware. The source and degree of light and the quality of the air both play a major part in determining the difference between comfort and discomfort, harmony and discord (see p. 88). Further elements, such as the use of colour, music, and plants, can, if well chosen, fuse into an environmental whole that will have a significant and cumulative influence on mood and behaviour. When decorating a room you should pay particular attention to the colour. This means not only being aware of the general effects of each colour, but also knowing your own preferences, since the effects of different colours vary from person to person.

Colour and mood

We are all colour biased. This is true whether you need to be enveloped by warm reds in order to relax and feel cheerful or whether you can only unwind fully surrounded by cool, whitewashed walls and pastel shades. Different colours have a subtle impact on mood and well-being. Blue and green tend to cool and calm, whereas red warms and stimulates. These effects may by physical as well as psychological. Experiments have shown that blue light can lead to a lowering of blood pressure while red light can cause blood pressure to increase. When used for interior design, some colours may unconsciously depress or elate, others may invigorate. This explains the popularity of neutral tones, such as white, cream, beige, and grey. You can use these as an overall background, introducing splashes of colour at will to please the eye.

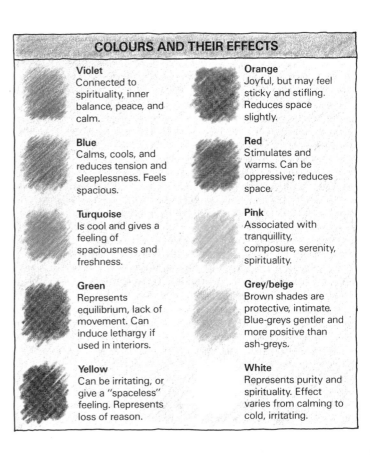

COLOURS AND THEIR EFFECTS

Violet
Connected to spirituality, inner balance, peace, and calm.

Blue
Calms, cools, and reduces tension and sleeplessness. Feels spacious.

Turquoise
Is cool and gives a feeling of spaciousness and freshness.

Green
Represents equilibrium, lack of movement. Can induce lethargy if used in interiors.

Yellow
Can be irritating, or give a "spaceless" feeling. Represents loss of reason.

Orange
Joyful, but may feel sticky and stifling. Reduces space slightly.

Red
Stimulates and warms. Can be oppressive; reduces space.

Pink
Associated with tranquillity, composure, serenity, spirituality.

Grey/beige
Brown shades are protective, intimate. Blue-greys gentler and more positive than ash-greys.

White
Represents purity and spirituality. Effect varies from calming to cold, irritating.

Light and air

Natural light is vital to us all. It regulates levels of the hormone melanonin, which has powerful effects on sleep, mood, and the reproductive cycle. Insufficient bright, natural daylight can cause a build-up of melanonin resulting in depression and lethargy. This is especially pronounced during winter when the condition is called "seasonal adaptive depression" (SAD). You can counteract it in a number of ways. Avoid fluorescent lighting, the most unnatural form of light. Work close to a window, go outside as often as you can on sunny days, and allow as much bright light as possible into your home. If you do have to stay inside in artificial light, buy full-spectrum lights, which simulate daylight.

Surroundings that are properly ventilated are essential to good health. The air contains electrically charged particles known as ions. Air that becomes charged with too many positive ions can cause lethargy and irritability, as well as physical illnesses such as asthma, hay fever, catarrh, and headaches. Positive ions build up in the atmosphere as a result of central heating, air conditioning, cigarette smoke, overcrowding, general pollution, and low barometric pressure. An ionizer will help keep the air in your home fresh and clear, charged with a continuous output of healthy, negative ions. This is especially useful if you cannot open the windows to improve ventilation–either because the outside temperature is too low or because of the design of the windows.

Air that is too dry may trigger sinus, throat, and respiratory disorders. You can use an electric humidifying unit to counteract this, but a simpler method is to place bowls of water in the room to maintain correct levels of humidity. The evaporation of moisture from plants, vases, and fish tanks will also help to maintain the balance.

The quality of the air is especially important in the bathroom, a room that is often unjustly neglected. Keep your bathroom warm and well ventilated, and try scenting it with fragrant candles, oils, or burning essence. Soft, warm, relaxing colours and flattering light will also help make your bathroom a more comfortable place in which it is pleasant and easy to relax.

Keep levels of humidity up by putting bowls of water around your home. Moisture from plants can also make the atmosphere more humid.

Furniture and health

Your body adapts very quickly to the furniture you use. A badly designed chair, a desk or worktop that is fraction too high or low, or a mattress which is either too hard or soft to support your weight, can all encourage faulty posture and compound the effects of physical strain and tension. This can happen before you even notice the discomfort. Slouched, stooped, and rigid movements and posture are common signs of this hidden, compensatory mechanism. Choose your furniture with care and forethought. Test it yourself thoroughly to make sure it meets your demands for support and comfort and you are more likely to avoid adaptive, postural stress. Pay particular attention to beds and mattresses. Your mattress should support every part of your back, yet mould itself to the contours of your body.

Choosing a chair

Any chair which you use for long periods of work must allow you to sit well back. Your back should be upright yet relaxed, providing support for the lower lumbar area. The edge of the seat must not cut into the backs of your thighs. You should be able to place your feet comfortably flat on the ground. Arms help relieve tension of the upper back.

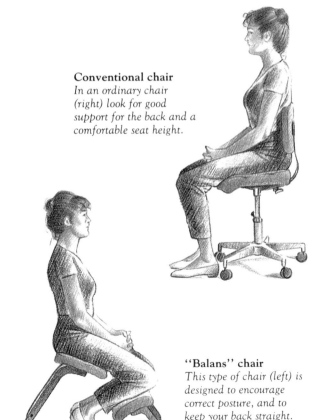

Conventional chair
*In an ordinary chair
(right) look for good
support for the back and a
comfortable seat height.*

"Balans" chair
*This type of chair (left) is
designed to encourage
correct posture, and to
keep your back straight.*

Nutrition and exercise

Food is the fuel that we take into our bodies and exercise creates the energy that uses up this fuel. They create a delicate balance. If you exercise too little and eat too much, you risk becoming overweight, while eating too little and exercising too much will also cause health problems. Until quite recently, our lifestyle allowed our energy input and output to be balanced automatically. We burnt up our calories to fuel body warmth and physical work.

But in today's consumer society most of us enjoy ample food, warmth, and comfort with minimum physical effort. Sedentary jobs, labour-saving devices in the home, automation in industry, and motorized transport, have led many of us to become less physically active, while relative affluence encourages us to follow a diet dominated by rich and fattening foods. The balance of energy supply and demand has been badly upset.

Controlling your diet and taking regular exercise will keep your weight at the right level and help protect you against illnesses such as diabetes and heart disease. It will also banish any stress that you are suffering as a direct result of being overweight.

Overweight can contribute to yet more serious problems. When linked to a high-stress, type A personality profile (see pages 40-44), to disorders such as high blood pressure and high blood cholesterol, or to habits such as smoking or drinking, being overweight can be a real health hazard. It will put an added strain on the heart, lungs, and other internal organs, with the effect of sapping energy, and lowering stamina.

It is relatively easy to control your weight by following a well-balanced and nutritious diet and exercising regularly. This may entail eating less or cutting back on certain foods when you gain a few extra pounds in weight. This chapter will help you work out which fattening foods to eliminate or reduce, and which nutritious, low-calorie foods you should replace them with. It also contains information on the main types of exercise to help you choose the best type for you.

The benefits of regular exerice are almost impossible to exaggerate. As well as promoting physical fitness and increased energy, exercise has an immediate effect on anxieties and worries. It is difficult to remain worried, angry, or anxious while your mind and body are engaged in physical activity. In addition, exercise is an ideal outlet for accumulated tension, bottled-up aggression, and frustration, neutralizing mental as well as muscular stress. People who exercise regularly claim some of the following benefits: improved sleep, fewer headaches, fewer stress-related aches and pains, a greater sense of inner calm, improved mental clarity and concentration, and greater physical stamina. Recent research shows that powerful brain chemicals are released during vigorous exercise. These are called endorphins, morphine-like substances associated with happiness and well-being. This is why exercise can often dispel negative mental states such as depression or anxiety. So combined together as part of your lifestyle, the right balance of diet and regular exercise can form the basis of a healthy, relaxed, and stress-proof life.

Assessing your diet

A varied, well-balanced diet is a basic cornerstone of healthy living, ensuring that mind and body have the opportunity to function at their peak levels. There is considerable controversy over exactly what makes up a well balanced diet. But the potential hazards of eating very large quantities of refined and processed foods, animal fats, dairy produce, and sugar are well documented, as are the health-giving properties of fresh fruit, vegetables, salads, grains, and wholefoods. There are also certain foods that affect your mood. Eaten in excess these can influence your stress level. So look at your diet and see if there are any deficiencies or types of food that you should cut down on. In particular, avoid "junk" foods and high-calorie snacks that give an instant energy "high". In the long run, these foods can damage your general health, depriving your body of essential nutrients. You will feel this effect most acutely at times of stress, so replace these foods with some of the healthy alternatives listed in this chapter.

Dietary deficiencies

You may think that you are getting enough variety in your diet, but you may still be losing out on essential nutrients. These can be lost for several reasons. Make sure your food is fresh. Once it gets to the shops, fresh food has an extremely short shelf life—nutrients such as vitamin C and the vitamin B group are rapidly destroyed or depleted through processing, storage, heat, and light. Overcooking also destroys nutrients. Eat as many raw vegetables as you can, and if you do cook them, do so minimally. Buy organically grown vegetables. Modern cultivation techniques can deprive fruit and vegetables of important nutrients. If you think your diet is deficient, look at the chart to see which elements might be missing.

SYMPTOMS OF DEFICIENCY

Symptom	Deficiency
Tiredness, anaemia	Lack of iron, vitamin B12
Colds, flu, infection	Lack of vitamin C
Cramps, irritability, PMT	Lack of B complex vitamins, calcium, magnesium
Dry skin, eczema, skin sores, bleeding gums	Lack of vitamin A, vitamin C, linoleic acid, polyunsaturated fat, zinc
Brittle, weak bones, aches in joints	Lack of vitamin D, calcium
Fatigue, weight gain (i.e. Thyroid imbalance)	Lack of iodine
Fluid retention (oedema)	Lack of potassium; excess salt
Migraine, dizziness, irritability, depression	Low blood sugar, insufficient protein and "complex carbohydrates"; excess sugar and sweet foods
Constipation, liverishness, irritable bowel syndrome	Lack of fibre; excess of refined, processed foods

MOOD FOODS

Food	Physical effects	Adverse reactions
Caffeine (in coffee, tea, aspirin, cola drinks)	Mimics stress arousal: direct stimulus of nervous system, increased alertness; stimulates heart, kidneys, adrenal glands; dilates blood vessels	Irritates kidneys; headaches, lethargy, irritability, muscular fatigue, nervousness, palpitations; these effects are especially bad when excessive intake is followed by withdrawal of tea or coffee
Sugar	Floods bloodstream giving instant energy high for short time and temporarily relieving physical tiredness	Adrenal glands overworked, making them less effective at regulating blood sugar levels; increased tiredness, depression, irritability.
Salt	Works with potassium to regulate the body's fluid balance	High blood pressure, nervousness, irritability when taken in excess; stimulates adrenal glands, stimulating stress arousal.
Tryptophan (amino acid present in chicken, fish, milk, bananas, pasta, rice)	Increases manufacture of the brain chemical serotonin, encouraging relaxation and sleepiness	Drowsiness if too many foods rich in tryptophan are eaten during the day.
Alcohol	Dilates blood vessels, raises blood sugar levels, relaxes body and mind, stimulates appetite and digestion	When taken in excess: liver damage, blood sugar problems, impaired judgement and brain function, poor co-ordination, depression, dependence on alcohol.

Food and mood

Some foods (above) influence emotions and behaviour patterns. The immediate effect of some is pleasant: alcohol, for example, makes most people feel relaxed quickly. But if you consume too much, alcohol, like the other substances in this chart, can reduce your body's ability to withstand stress.

Food supplements

Tailor your diet to your lifestyle (right). If you are under a great deal of stress or emotional trauma, you are likely to need more of the B complex vitamins, vitamin C, and minerals such as zinc, which the body uses up more quickly under stress. This also applies to people who smoke, drink a lot of alcohol, take antibiotics, or are on the contraceptive pill.

FOOD SUPPLEMENTS

Supplement	Condition
Vitamin C	Colds; after excessive intake of alcohol; when smoking cigarettes
Vitamin B6	PMT; taking the contraceptive pill, antibiotics; times of tension and prolonged stress
Oil of evening primrose	PMT; during excessive intake of alcohol; cigarette smoking; eczema
Lysine	Cold sores, eczema, psoriasis
Iron plus vitamin B12	Tiredness; iron-deficiency anaemia; heavy periods
Dolomite, calcium, magnesium, vitamin B6	Insomnia, irritability, muscular cramp
Brewer's yeast (rich in B complex vitamins)	Stress, excess alcohol intake, smoking cigarettes, contraceptive pill, antibiotics
Feverfew	Migraine
Zinc plus vitamin E	Burns, wounds

The stress-free diet

The idea of changing your diet to strengthen your body's defences against stress is not a new one. Fasting, purification régimes, and the dietary principles of yoga all aim to cleanse the body, eliminate harmful toxins, and allow the internal organs to rest and recuperate. The result should be a stronger body and increased energy–both mental and physical. A healthy diet should consist of several elements. Among the most important are fresh fruit, vegetables, and fibre. If you eat meat, make sure it is lean, or remove the fat before cooking. Many of the foods we rely on at times of stress and tiredness are themselves stress-inducing. But there are healthy alternatives to most of them, many of which are more palatable than their stress-inducing counterparts. Your attitude is as important for your health as what you actually eat. Always put time aside to enjoy your food and eat slowly, savouring each mouthful. Don't eat while reading, cooking, talking on the telephone, or working. If you tend to eat more when you are depressed, watch out for the signs and try doing something completely different–do some exercise, relax with a book, or visit a friend. And, above all, whenever you eat–enjoy your food.

Fruit
This makes a good alternative to pies and puddings. Try fresh or dried fruit with yoghurt or lightly stewed fruit, sprinkled with muesli and honey for extra flavour.

Vegetables
Eat vegetables raw or very lightly steamed or boiled to keep in the nutrients. Raw vegetables add a variety of colour, texture, and taste to a meal. Make up as many meals as you can from a selection of two or three different vegetables. You should also experiment with new salad combinations: try mixtures of fruit, nuts, and raw vegetables. The latter will add a variety of different textures, colours, and tastes.

Fibre
Eat some fibre every day. The following foods are fibre-rich: whole-wheat flour, bread and pasta, brown rice, sweetcorn, beans and pulses, potatoes with their skins, and raw vegetables.

HEALTHY ALTERNATIVES

Food group	Foods	Alternatives
Sweet foods	Biscuits, jams, cakes, chocolates, sweets, sugared cereals, cocoa, sweet drinks, honeys, relishes, puddings, pies, processed foods containing hidden sugar	Sugar-free jam, apple butter, apple and pear spread, blackstrap molasses, muesli, aspartamine sugar substitute, carob chocolate substitute, raisins, dates, figs, dried fruit, fresh fruit juices.
Saturated/animal fats	Fatty red meat, pork, bacon, sausages, hamburgers, lard, suet dripping, hard margarine, full-fat milk, cream, full-fat yoghurt, fried food, butter, full-fat cheese, hidden fats in sauces, dressings, soups	Lean chicken, fish, game, polyunsaturated vegetable oils and margarines, skimmed milk, low-fat yoghurt, cottage cheese, goat's milk cheese.
Processed/refined foods	White flour, white rice, white bread, pre-packed foods, all foods in the "sweet" category	Brown rice, wholewheat flour, rye, barley, corn, oats, buckwheat; wholemeal bread, pasta, and rice; pulses, beans, wholegrain cereals.
Salt	Chips, crisps, salted nuts, processed foods that use salt as a preservative	Raw unsalted nuts, pumpkin seeds, sunflower seeds, raw vegetables, seaweed.
Caffeine	Coffee, tea, cola drinks, some painkillers	Herbal teas, decaffeinated coffee, dandelion coffee, fresh vegetable and fruit juices, spring water.

Avoiding unhealthy foods

The modern diet contains several groups of foods which, though unhealthy, many of us feel we cannot do without. There are healthy alternatives to most of these. Many taste similar to the foods they replace; most are actually more appetizing–try the healthy alternatives and you will probably end up preferring them on grounds of taste alone. Beware of unhealthy foods when you are eating out and the choice is limited. At parties, steer clear of nuts, cheese, biscuits, and canapés. Instead, fill up with vegetables, such as celery, radishes, and carrot sticks.

Meat and fish

Buy lean meat and trim off any surplus fat before cooking. Grilling, spit-roasting, and baking in aluminium foil are the best cooking methods for meat. Remove chicken skin before cooking as this is high in fat. Cook fish simply, avoiding heavy sauces–grill it or bake it in foil. Oily fish such as mackerel, herring, and salmon are a good source of beneficial unsaturated fatty acids.

Which exercise for you?

Exercise, like food, should give pleasure as well as do you good. This is why it is important to find an activity that suits your individual personality, schedule, and physical capabilities. The appeal of skilled sports, such as tennis, golf, or football, is obviously greater if you have spent some time learning the game and have developed a certain proficiency. But most sports need time and effort, and this often means that if you lead a busy life it is difficult to do them regularly. In addition, highly competitive sports like squash can add an extra load of stress to an already demanding lifestyle. So for many people, a better choice is a form of non-competitive exercise, such as swimming, cycling, walking, or calisthenics.

Once you begin, do not push yourself too hard, and if you have any health problems (past or present), check with your doctor about which type of exercise you can take up safely. It is better to exercise regularly for short periods than to do a lot of exercise infrequently or irregularly. All-out, marathon exercise sessions done without proper training bring risks of injury, fatigue, or total exhaustion.

Use the charts on the following pages to help you decide which form of exercise is the one for you. The exercises have been divided up into six categories. Aerobic dance and other forms of aerobic exercise work by increasing the body's consumption of oxygen, raising the heart rate and making the arteries and lungs expand. Calisthenics include the body management exercises featured in chapter 10 of this book, while yoga is covered in chapter 12. For the other two forms of exercise, martial arts (judo, aikido, karate, and t'ai chi) and weight machines, you will need access to special facilities. You will find weight machines in your local health club or gym, while expert tuition over a long period is required for the martial arts. Each chart is divided up for ease of reference. Under "Key facts" you will find basic information about how each type of exercise works, what you need to do it, and how much time is required. "Body confidence" covers the psychological benefits, "Recommended" describes the types of people to whom the exercise is best suited, and the fitness benefits are given in the final column.

Make your choice of exercise by using the tables on the following pages.

AEROBIC DANCE

Key facts	Body confidence	Fitness benefits
How it works Combines dance steps, calisthenics, running in place, hopping, and jumping, all set to music; borrows from many different types of dance. **What you need** Shorts and T-shirt or leotard and tights, comfortable and not too tight fitting. A space about 9 × 12 ft (3 × 4 m), plus an instruction book and record or a video cassette. Or you can join a class. **Time required** Classes usually run for 1 hour twice a week.	Exercising to music and learning routines can lift the spirits and boost confidence. You can expect improvements in balance, stride, posture, and body image. **Recommended** If you think you are unathletic, artistic, or musical. Classes appeal if you are sociable and like working with a teacher. **Note** Avoid if you have disorder of the foot, knee, back, or ankle.	**Flexibility** A good programme will increase flexibility through 10–20 mins of warm-up and stretching exercises. **Strength** Abdominal muscles are strengthened by sit-ups and leg raises, legs with running and kicks. There are usually no exercises to increase upper-body strength. **Cardiovascular endurance** Classes usually include 20–30 mins continuous jumping, dancing, and jogging for cardiovascular endurance.

AEROBIC EXERCISE

Key facts	Body confidence	Fitness benefits
How it works Sustained running, fast walking, swimming, or cycling increases your consumption of oxygen, raising your heart rate, and expanding your lungs and arteries. Done regularly, this form of exercise speeds up the metabolism and the rate at which you burn up calories, even when at rest. **What you need** A track suit, shorts, and sweat shirt, and training shoes for running. **Time required** 10-20 mins daily.	Increased endurance and strength offer good benefits here. Testing your personal best by recording distances and timings and extending your limits improves self-image. **Recommended** If you like simple exercises that you can do outdoors and that take only a short time; if you like exercising alone; if your competitive spirit is low. **Note** Avoid if you have a physical weakness or injury.	**Flexibility** Do five minutes' stretching and flexing exercises before and after running to avoid injury and promote flexibility. Cycling and swimming improve muscle flexibility. **Strength** Excellent improvements are possible, especially in the strength of the legs and hips. **Cardiovascular endurance** Aerobic exercise is second to none in strengthening your heart and lungs and improving overall stamina.

CALISTHENICS

Key facts	Body confidence	Fitness benefits
How it works Uses general keep-fit exercises that stretch and tone the muscles without using equipment. They are useful on their own or before sports. **What you need** Leotard and tights, a track suit, or shorts and T-shirt. Beginners should consider joining a class, although a book of exercises can start you off, or keep you going later. **Time required** A 30–40 min session, preferably daily. Pre-sport calisthenics take 10–20 mins.	Stretching and toning of the muscles improves alignment, posture, and stride. **Recommended** If you are self-disciplined and like to exercise on your own; if you are on a rigid schedule, since you can do calisthenics anywhere; if you like mechanical, non-taxing exercise.	**Flexibility** Stretching calisthenic exercises can greatly improve all-over flexibility. **Strength** Calisthenics build your strength, although not as quickly as using weights. **Cardiovascular endurance** If supplemented with a programme of running or jumping rope, calisthenics can improve cardiovascular endurance.

YOGA

Key facts	Body confidence	Fitness benefits
How it works Uses postures, held for a sustained period, for attaining mental and physical balance and well-being. **What you need** Loose, comfortable clothing or leotard and tights. Classes are given by experienced teachers. Once you have learned the basics, a book of yoga exercises will help you. **Time required** A yoga session should last at least 30 mins, and be done at least three times a week. Classes last $1-1\frac{1}{2}$ hours.	Yoga emphasizes body awareness and so encourages physical self-respect; it helps you to become more aware of body function and posture. **Recommended** If you have problems with muscular tension; if you lead a pressured, highly stressed life; if you want exercise for the mind as well as the body; if you cannot do vigorous physical activity; if you are patient.	**Flexibility** One of the main aims of yoga is to improve flexibility by stretching and toning all parts of the body. **Strength** Holding postures increase muscle strength only minimally. Some programmes also include strength exercises to make up for this lack. **Cardiovascular endurance** Yoga does little for cardiovascular endurance.

WEIGHT MACHINES

Key facts	Body confidence	Fitness benefits
How it works The machines hold the weights and you work the movable parts. There are machines for nearly every muscle group. **What you need** Access to a set of weight machines. This means joining a health club or gym. Wear a sweat suit or shorts, T-shirt and sneakers. **Time required** About 30 mins three times a week. Longer or more frequent work-outs are counterproductive because of muscle fatigue.	Seeing steady improvements in the amount of weight you can lift is rewarding. **Recommended** If you want visible results quickly; if you like indoor exercise in a club atmosphere with the advantage of working alone; if you can afford club fees.	**Flexibility** This improves if you use the machines correctly, extending the muscles fully before each move. **Strength** This is the main benefit of using weight machines. **Cardiovascular endurance** The gain here is minimal. Add some jogging, cycling, or swimming if you want an improvement in cardiovascular endurance.

MARTIAL ARTS

Key facts	Body confidence	Fitness benefits
How it works These forms of eastern self-defence training teach a range of manoeuvres – kicks, punches, and holds. T'ai chi is slower and dance like. **What you need** An outfit called a gi, consisting of pants, jacket, and belt. For t'ai chi, loose-fitting clothing and comfortable shoes. You must attend a class. **Time required** Classes take 1–2 hours and should be taken at least twice a week for several years.	A major benefit. The martial arts promote physical and emotional self-awareness and foster self-defence expertise. **Recommended** If you are adventurous and prepared for the long-term commitment required; if you want a discipline that involves a lot of body contact and physicality; if you want to develop your self-defence capability.	**Flexibility** Most programmes include stretching exercises, aiding the flexibility required for high kicks and other movements. **Strength** Karate and judo usually incorporate strength-building exercises including push-ups and sit-ups. **Cardiovascular endurance** Most types (except t'ai chi) spend a lot of time on routines that exercise the heart.

WAYS TO RELAX

Relaxation techniques

Relaxation is the most natural activity in the world. Animals retain an in-built capacity for alternating periods of physical tension with regular states of relaxation in a way that we humans have long forgotten. Look at the way a cat stretches its limbs, or sensuously arches its back, how a dog yawns and flops on its back, its paws hanging loose. We have a lot to learn from the way animals release pent-up tension from their bodies or ease themselves into action. Why should we treat our own bodies with any less sense and sensibility?

Yet relaxation is a forgotten art. Few people today could claim to be completely relaxed for most of their waking hours. It says something about the degree of stress in our lives, the amount of unconscious or hidden tension in our bodies, that we need to relearn and practise the art of relaxation in order to safeguard our well-being.

For relaxation to be effective, we need to banish tension from both mind and body. Ideally speaking a good night's sleep should perform this function. But there is no guarantee that it will, and although we do spend a lot of our sleeping time—though by no means all of it—in a relaxed state, sleep alone is not enough. Today, when we are continuously bombarded by stress-inducing stimuli, we need to develop our skills in conscious relaxation as much as possible.

Many people do not realise how unrelaxed they really are. If you have started to ignore the build-up of strain and tension in your limbs, joints, and muscles, and fail to defuse these physical stresses when they begin to affect your mind and body, you will gradually begin to store that tension in various parts of your body. You will be carrying tension around with you whatever you do. Allowing hidden tension to increase and take hold of your body will inevitably affect the way that you feel and how you function, since a tense body is less efficient and well co-ordinated than a relaxed one. You will also start to feel the physical effects of stress—a broad gamut of aches and pains from migraine headaches to back pain.

There are two immediate advantages of learning to relax. Firstly, as you begin to practise relaxation techniques you will become aware at once of the areas of your body that are most prone to stiffness and pain. This can help keep you on your guard against factors that may exacerbate the strain—your posture, your furniture, the shoes and clothes you wear, and the way you use your body in general. Secondly, you will simply feel much better—almost immediately. Five minutes spent loosening your face, neck, and shoulder muscles may banish a headache and leave you feeling calm and refreshed, while twenty minutes' deeper relaxation can rest and revive both mind and body as much as two hours' sleep.

A few of the exercises in this chapter are strenuous—do not worry, if you cannot do them at first. But most are early and yield fast benefits.

Unlike the sluggish torpor we drift into in bed at night, conscious relaxation consists of learning systematically to empty the mind and muscles of stress and external stimuli through a series of deliberately disciplined, progressive exercises.

Relaxation and the body

When we are truly relaxed, very definite and measurable changes take place in the body. These changes distinguish relaxation from the opposite states of tension or arousal. Some of the most significant changes are triggered by the two branches of the autonomic nervous system. The sympathetic branch of the nervous system slows down. This branch controls body temperature, digestion, heart rate, respiratory rate, blood flow and pressure, and muscular tension. Conversely, the opposite, parasympathetic, branch of the nervous system comes increasingly into play. This lowers oxygen consumption and reduces the following bodily functions: carbon dioxide elimination, heart and respiratory rates, blood pressure, blood lactate, and blood cortisol levels. It also reduces muscle tone, and activates the internal organs to work more efficiently. These bodily changes are collectively referred to by doctors as the "relaxation response". This is the reverse of the aroused "fight or flight" response with which we react to stress.

Alpha plus theta
rhythms
(meditation)

Relaxation and the brain

The activity of the brain can provide vital information about how relaxed you are. The brain emits four different types of waves, each with its own characteristic rhythm. These are beta, the ordinary conscious day-to-day rhythms; delta, present when we sleep and dream; theta, which reflect a withdrawn, dreamlike state; and alpha, which are associated with deep physical relaxation and emotional tranquillity, when the mind is calm yet still awake and alert. Very deep relaxation and meditation induce a predominance of alpha and theta rhythms, indicating a state of harmony. It is possible to measure these waves by using biofeedback equipment, and many doctors and therapists use this technique as a way of monitoring how relaxed we are.

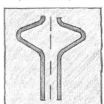

Theta rhythms
(dreaming sleep).

Recent research also suggests that among the biochemical changes triggered by relaxation there is an increase in the body's manufacture of certain mood-altering chemicals (known as neurotransmitters). In particular the body's production of serotonin, which is associated principally with feelings of calmness and happiness, is increased.

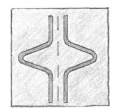

Alpha rhythms
(between waking
and sleep)

Readouts from biofeedback monitoring equipment show how meditation induces both alpha and theta rhythms–indicating a state of calmness.

Choosing relaxation exercises

The exercises illustrated in this chapter are simple to learn and to carry out. They are designed to be done either as a complete top-to-toe series, or singly, depending on how much time you have and what your individual requirements are. Some will help you get rid of tension in specific parts of your body. Others will give a more general relaxation, producing a calming effect like that of meditation.

The busier and more stressed you are, the more you should incorporate relaxation techniques into your daily schedule. Don't wait until you are racked with back pain or laid low by headaches or muscle spasms. Relaxation exercises are an ideal way of waking up and flexing the muscles after sleep to ease away early-morning stiffness. You can also use these exercises as a mid-morning or afternoon break to relieve tension at work, while in the evening they can help dispel fatigue. Another way to use these exercises—especially the more strenuous ones like those for the neck, back, and shoulders—is to do them at night to help you to go to sleep. If you do them regularly they will eventually become second nature and essential to your mental and physical well-being.

If you are too busy to do the whole series, or if you feel that you need to relax one particular part of your body, then you will still find that doing one or two exercises will help you relax. For example, if tension is building up in your head and neck, you may choose to do only the exercises that cover this area. If you feel generally tense, but do not have time to do all the exercises, try one or more of the general exercises at the end of the chapter (see pages 112-13). One of the most effective is to lie on the floor and progressively tense and let go, stretch and release, each and every part of the body. This exercise is deeply relaxing and helps you to recognise and distinguish between the different sensations of tension and relaxation. Allow plenty of time for this exercise and concentrate your mind on feelings of heaviness and warmth in your limbs while keeping your breathing smooth. Whether you do one exercise or a whole series, remember that you will obtain the most lasting benefit if you exercise regularly, at the same time every day.

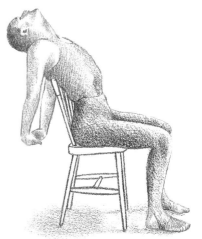

Head and neck exercises

Do these head, neck, and face exercises as often as you can. They will keep the muscles supple and help prevent both physical and mental tension. Tiredness and tension in the head area can be a particular problem if you have to sit and work at a desk for long periods, or if you spend a lot of time standing and talking. Tension can lodge in the back of the neck and this in turn causes constriction of the small muscles and blood vessels of the scalp, temples, and hairline. Headaches and migraine are obvious warnings. Tightness of the throat, eyestrain, numbness, and cricks in the neck are also symptoms of this type of tension.

Head rolls
Roll your head slowly clockwise and then counter-clockwise, three times each way, allowing it to drop heavily.

Head and neck

Head rolls and neck stretches ease away deep-rooted tension. To make them more effective practise them as slowly as possible to maximize the stretch. Moving the head too rapidly when you are tense can increase stiffness and cause twinges and cricks. Each time you drop the head feel its complete weight and allow your jaw to open and your eyes to close so that the relaxing effects are increased.

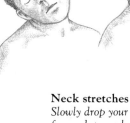

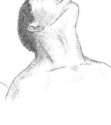

Neck stretches
Slowly drop your head forward, to each side, and backward, as far as possible, stretching the neck muscles. Repeat ten times.

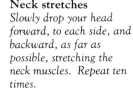

Turning the head
Keeping your head level, turn it side to side ten times slowly, then ten times more quickly.

Neck and shoulders

If you do this exercise correctly you should feel the pull along the top and back of your shoulders each time you shrug. Alternate shrugging movements with shoulder rolls, rotating shoulders back then forward ten times. Keep your hands and arms completely limp.

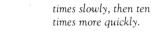
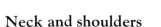

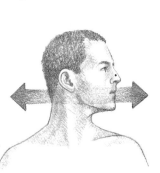

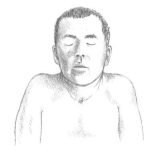

Shrug both shoulders together and each alternately. Raise them high and let them drop heavily.

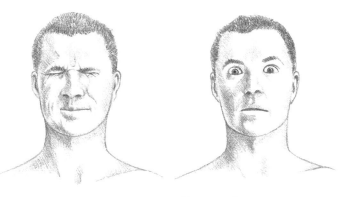

Face and jaw

This is the most overlooked area of the body when it comes to relaxation, since few of us think we need to exercise the face. Yet the face has a number of tension spots, often linked to stiffness of the neck and head. Strain may become locked into the tiny muscles around the mouth, lips, and the vertical and horizontal forehead muscles, while concentrating for long periods can tire and strain the eye area. Another stress target is the mouth, tongue and jaw, in particular the joint connecting the upper and lower jaw. This may slip out of alignment causing pain in the head, face or back, toothache, neuralgia, or eye problems. Practise face and neck exercises whenever you have few minutes to spare alone in front of a mirror.

Eye exercises

1 *Close both eyes; tighten the surrounding muscles into a screwed-up expression for ten seconds.*
2 *Open your eyes wide and relax the facial muscles for a count of ten.*

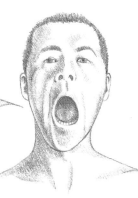

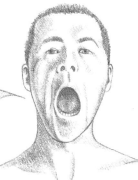

Jaw movements

1 *With mouth shut or open, shift your jaw gently but firmly from left to right ten times.*

2 *Alternatively, drop the lower jaw as far as possible and open your mouth wide.*

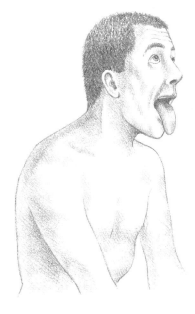

Facial exercise

Begin with a relaxed expression. Then open your mouth wide, stick out your tongue and, opening your eyes very wide, try to "see" the tip of your tongue by focusing the eyes inward.

Neck, back, and shoulder exercises

Shoulder tension and backache are very common and have many causes. Deskbound jobs and poor posture are two of the main factors Heavy lifting can also result in back strain, especially if you bend forward with straight legs to pick up heavy objects off the floor. Women who wear very high heels most of the day or regularly carry heavy shopping with one arm risk distorting the alignment of back and shoulders. Swap bags from side to side and wear the strap of your shoulder bag diagonally across your upper body. Release tension from shoulders, neck, and back as soon as you feel it.

Neck and shoulders

There is no set time or rhythm for these upper body exercises. Do them as slowly as you wish, and stay bent over for as long as you feel you need to relax. Try to feel the contrast between the upward stretch and the heaviness of a completely relaxed upper body as you drop forward from the hips.

1 Stand upright, your feet about twelve inches apart and parallel, your arms stretched above your head.

2 Allow your upper body to drop forward from the hips, keeping the knees relaxed or slightly bent. Let the arms, head, and shoulders hang relaxed for up to forty seconds.

3 Shake out the arms and shoulders, nod and shake the head, then slowly raise the body. Repeat a few times.

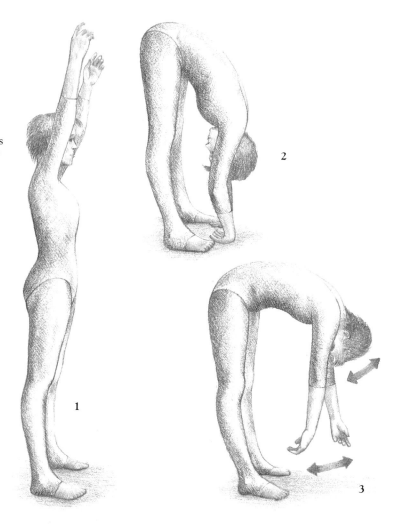

Neck and shoulders

Choose a chair with a firm seat
and a hard, upright back and
make sure you can place your
feet firmly on the floor. Either
do the exercise once, staying
rolled over for as long as you
can, or practise it more rhythmically, 2-5 times.

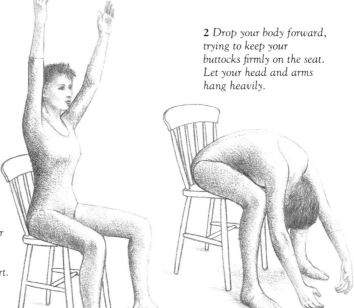

*2 Drop your body forward,
trying to keep your
buttocks firmly on the seat.
Let your head and arms
hang heavily.*

*1 Sit upright, with your
lower back supported by
the chair, and stretch your
arms and trunk upward.
Keep your feet parallel
about 20 ins (50 cm) apart.*

Backstretch

For this exercise you need a
chair with a firm, upright back
that comes up to shoulderblade
level. Don't worry if at first
you cannot stretch back very
far. As tension and tightness in
the shoulders and upper arms
eases you will be able to stretch
further and gain more pliability.
Do the movements slowly but
with no set rhythm.

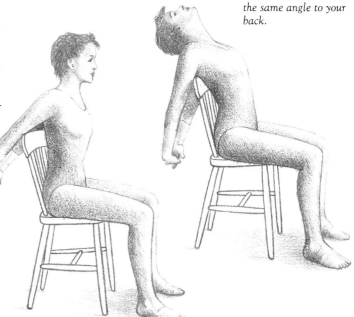

*2 Gradually lean
backward, arching your
upper back over the chair.
Try to keep your arms at
the same angle to your
back.*

*1 Slowly raise your arms
behind the back of the
chair clasping the hands
firmly. Squeeze your
shoulder blades together.*

Spine and lower back exercises

Lower backache is by far the most common back problem. It can be due to incorrect posture, badly designed furniture, beds that are too hard or too soft, pregnancy, menstruation, weight gain, and lack of exercise. Practise these gentle stretching and curling exercises every day to relieve pressure on the spine and to prevent as well as alleviate stiffness. Never push or pull your back into any position, but ease yourself very gradually and gently into a position that feels comfortable and provides a pleasurable stretching sensation. Stop if you feel you any strain. These exercises also provide a good warm up and cool down before and after a more hectic exercise session.

Foetal roll

Most of us naturally adopt the foetal, curled-up pose if we have a tense or aching back. But pulling the knees up to the chest gives a fuller stretch and relieves tension faster. Do this exercise either on the floor or in bed before going to sleep. You can also do it on waking if your back gets stiff at this time.

Backstretch

Gaining sufficient flexibility to do this exercise takes time and perseverance until the muscles become used to being stretched. Concentrate all the time on relaxing your hips, inner thighs, and upper back muscles.

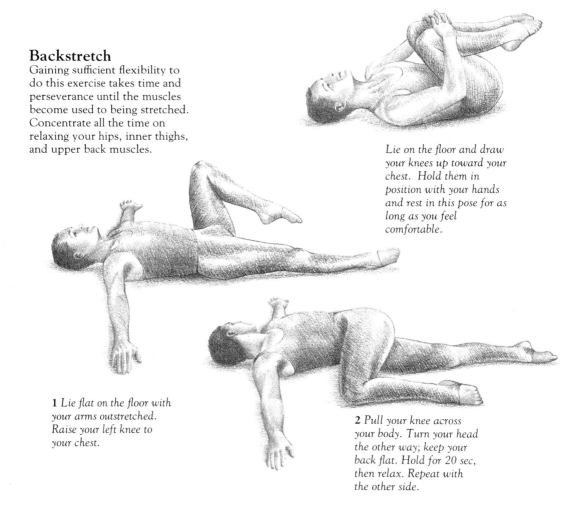

Lie on the floor and draw your knees up toward your chest. Hold them in position with your hands and rest in this pose for as long as you feel comfortable.

1 *Lie flat on the floor with your arms outstretched. Raise your left knee to your chest.*

2 *Pull your knee across your body. Turn your head the other way; keep your back flat. Hold for 20 sec, then relax. Repeat with the other side.*

Warm-up

This simple technique eases tension in the lower and middle back by gently stretching the spine. It also increases the flexibility of the hip joints as well as encouraging the stretch of the groin muscles. Tightness of the hips and groin automatically creates tension in the lower back and vice-versa. Do this exercise in your own time and don't rush the forward stretch. Grasp the ankles and pull yourself over very slowly and gently without straining the muscles.

1 Sit upright, hands clasping your ankles and your knees bent.

2 Slowly bend forward. Try to place your head on your feet. Hold, then sit up. Repeat five times.

Facing Mecca

Think of a cat when you practise this yoga-type backstretch, which is designed to relieve tension along the entire length of the spine. Your head should remain relaxed while your arms feel as if you are reaching forward as far as you can. Do not allow your bottom and lower spine to rise up and concentrate on pressing your back into the floor.

Kneel with your body upright and your arms resting at your sides. Lower your buttocks onto your heels, then pull your body forward as shown above. Rest in this pose for as long as you wish.

Leg and foot exercises

Healthy feet, leg muscles, and knee joints are essential for balance, mobility, and good posture. Unless you walk a lot or exercise regularly these can all stiffen up and lose their strength and tone. When sitting for long periods keep moving your legs slightly to avoid tiredness. Avoid tight-fitting footwear and high-heeled shoes. These press on the muscles, ligaments, and bones, reducing mobility and blood flow, and distorting the structure of the foot. This can result in fatigue and can also cause corns, callouses, and bunions. So wherever you are, walk around barefoot or wear exercise sandals as much as possible.

Relaxing the feet
Through wearing shoes that are very tight or have high heels, we tend to lose contact with the true feel of the ground. Restrictive footwear also cramps the foot muscles, causes distortion, stiffness and aches, and even affects our balance and movement. You should always do foot and leg exercises without shoes and socks. Try to savour the contact of bare flesh on carpet or wood and concentrate on keeping the toes as far apart as possible. Wiggle them around and separate them into a fan shape from time to time to increase mobility and relieve stiffness. Do this exercise slowly and rhythmically to exercise your legs and feet.

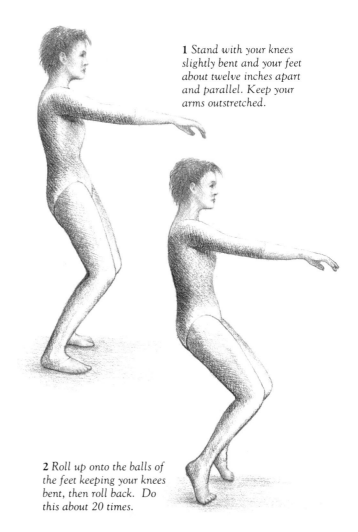

1 *Stand with your knees slightly bent and your feet about twelve inches apart and parallel. Keep your arms outstretched.*

2 *Roll up onto the balls of the feet keeping your knees bent, then roll back. Do this about 20 times.*

Ankle rolls

Tension accumulates in the ankle joints, the front of the calves, and the foot muscles. This happens especially if you do not exercise regularly, spend a lot of time sitting or standing, or wear restricting shoes. Fluid retention, especially in women, can aggravate stiffness and discomfort in the feet. It can be caused by PMT, long-distance air travel, a faulty diet, and poor circulation. Take off your shoes and wiggle your toes then roll your ankles whenever and wherever you can.

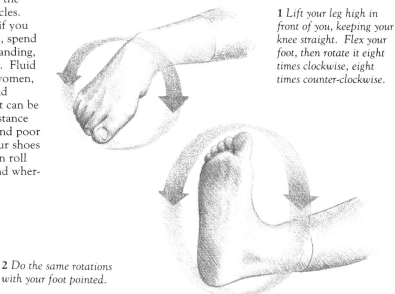

1 Lift your leg high in front of you, keeping your knee straight. Flex your foot, then rotate it eight times clockwise, eight times counter-clockwise.

2 Do the same rotations with your foot pointed.

Relaxing the knees

Long periods of inactivity, tiredness, even anger and irritability, cause tension to lodge in the muscles and ligaments surrounding the knee. Leg kicks will help relax the knees. Do them barefoot or wearing gym-shoes–this will allow you to shake off the accumulated tension. Don't try to kick too high, and let the leg relax immediately after the kick.

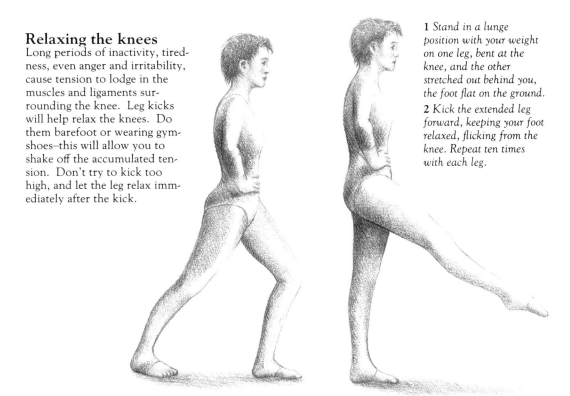

1 Stand in a lunge position with your weight on one leg, bent at the knee, and the other stretched out behind you, the foot flat on the ground.

2 Kick the extended leg forward, keeping your foot relaxed, flicking from the knee. Repeat ten times with each leg.

General exercises

Shaking out the body or letting it flop and hang are excellent ways to dispel both mental strain and physical tension. Hanging from a door frame or parallel bar is also surprisingly relaxing. The weight of your body gently disimpacts the vertebrae, easing out tight muscles and ligaments. Letting your body go completely limp like a rag doll, or systematically tightening or flexing each part of the body and then relaxing it, helps to focus your mind on the very different sensations of strain and relaxation, producing a calming effect similar to simple meditation or autosuggestion. As you do these exercises, feel the lightness of your limbs and try to visualize what your body looks like when relaxed.

Hanging from the hands
Grasp hold of a doorframe or parallel bar and stretch your body, making sure the feet do not rest on the floor. Just hang there–don't swing.

Hanging from a bar
Try and relax each part of your body fully while inverted or while hanging from your arms. Hanging upside-down or the right way up will stretch and relax most of the major muscle groups and joints, and gives your spine an ultimate stretch. Stop if you start to feel dizzy or sick, or if you develop cramp. Never hang upside down with a full stomach. If you cannot find a suitable parallel bar or a door frame that allows you to clear the floor with your feet as you hang, find a board the same length as your body, prop it up at as steep an incline as possible, and lie on it, head downward.

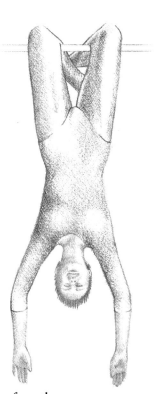

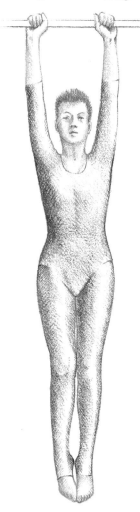

Hanging from the knees
Hook your knees over a bar and let your body hang limp for anything from two to ten minutes.

Hanging loose

You can think of this as the rag-doll jog. Run either on the spot, or anywhere out of doors. Keep your body completely relaxed and your mind clear of distracting thoughts. If you wish, use extra movements to make this exercise more interesting. Try hopping from side to side with your feet close together, or dropping your upper body right down to your knees as you jog, then rising up again, allowing your arms to swing around more freely. If you get a stitch you are probably not as fully relaxed as you should be.

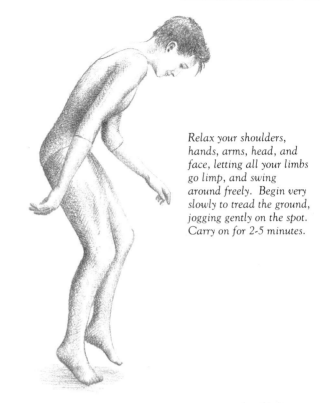

Relax your shoulders, hands, arms, head, and face, letting all your limbs go limp, and swing around freely. Begin very slowly to tread the ground, jogging gently on the spot. Carry on for 2-5 minutes.

Flat out

Lying or sitting, quietly isolating tension spots and becoming aware of the difference between tension and relaxation in various parts of the body is one of the best first steps to relaxation. By systematically either flexing or tightening the muscles, starting from the toes and feet and working all the way up to the facial muscles, and then totally relaxing them, you will start to become aware of knots of tightness and strain you may never have known existed.

Lie flat on the floor, close your eyes, and relax. Alternately tighten each muscle group and then relax it. When you are completely relaxed, lie for a further five minutes, savouring the feeling.

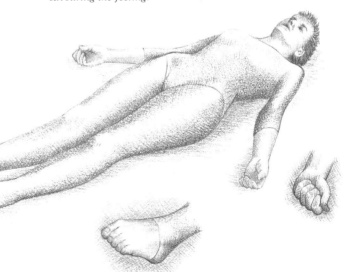

Body management

When you are in good physical shape, you will be able to take stress in your stride. Your body will become a well tuned and highly expressive instrument, through which you can project your personality and feelings, an accurate sensor that will register physical stimuli and emotions. Being unfit will not only make it more difficult for you to withstand or cope with the effects of stress. It will also add to the amount of stress you experience because of tension in your body. This in turn will interfere with your co-ordination and agility, and may cause aches and pains.

The most effective body-management or body-conditioning techniques can unburden the human body of years of accumulated stresses and strains reflected by faulty posture and lack of physical awareness. But they have other benefits. They can remove the straitjacketing effects of past illnesses, emotional shocks, or traumas, and help you identify unresolved negative emotions such as anger or depression which are often locked into certain parts of the body, distorting and limiting its freedom of movement.

These techniques also help improve your posture. This is something to which most people are largely oblivious. But bad posture is guaranteed to load the body with extra tension and stress. It is revealed by shallow or erratic breathing, clumsy gestures, stilted body rhythms, and even strained facial expressions. Yet hunched shoulders, a stooped, tense back, a rigid neck and head, and a slumped abdominal area, can creep upon us unawares and become second nature. Eventually these will lead to physical weakness and strain, and increase the risk of injury especially to the back. In fact the back is the first part of you that suffers if you develop faulty posture. Often linked with other stress-related ailments, back pain affects eight out of ten adults and is the major cause of absence from work in America and Europe today.

Playing sports or exercising does not necessarily guarantee a well co-ordinated, relaxed body. Vigorous exercise can often "work-in" posture defects and accentuated isolated problems and pains. To establish if yours is a truly well integrated body, ask yourself whether it has five key characteristics: strength, suppleness, agility, co-ordination, and balance. These qualities can be cultivated by practising one of the bodywork systems or body therapies such as Medau, Feldenkrais, Pilates, T'ai chi, or Mensendieck (see pages 188-9). These systems will realign, strengthen, and stretch the body within the limits of its own individual capability. The exercises in this chapter are designed to help you become more aware of the prime areas of postural defect and strain, and to encourage improved body consciousness. If you find any of them too difficult, start by doing only part of the exercise, and avoid strain.

You cannot completely isolate and work on one part of the body without affecting others. Posture is a chain of cause and effect, complete with weak links and stresses. So be conscious of the entire body when exercising any part of it: all the limbs and organs are linked and interdependent, so strain and misplacement in one area of the body will inevitably be reflected in another.

Arms and chest

Exercises that expand the chest not only improve breathing and increase lung capacity. They also relieve strain and tension in the upper back. This is very important because weak chest and arm muscles can put extra strain on the back when you lift or carry heavy objects. Remember when practising these exercises to hold your back upright, keeping your neck in alignment with your spine, relaxing your shoulders and neck. As an alternative to the exercises in this chapter, swimming or using dumb bells strengthen the chest muscles, increasing stamina and lifting power in the biceps and triceps.

Circling

If your arms are very weak it may take time until you are able to circle them continuously and rapidly without tiring the muscles. Make sure you do not bend your elbows while circling. Keep your chest expanded and your spine erect. Your body should remain still while you rotate your arms rhythmically and smoothly. Do not jerk the movements.

Backstroke

The backstroke in swimming is one of the best exercises for strengthening the arms, loosening tension, and expanding the chest. Simulate it by co-ordinating your arm movements and keeping the arms as close to your head as possible.

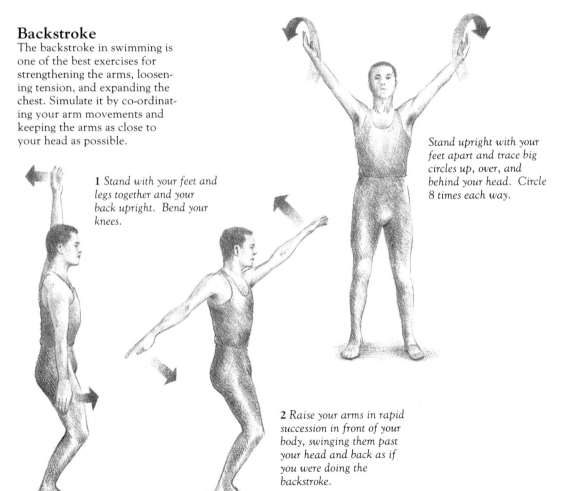

1 Stand with your feet and legs together and your back upright. Bend your knees.

Stand upright with your feet apart and trace big circles up, over, and behind your head. Circle 8 times each way.

2 Raise your arms in rapid succession in front of your body, swinging them past your head and back as if you were doing the backstroke.

Lateral movements

Working the arms laterally exercises the front and tops of the shoulders as well as the upper arms themselves. Accumulated tension and strain can reduce strength in this area by making the muscles contract, while hunching or slouching of the shoulders narrows the chest, restricting lung capacity and generally weakening the upper body. Relax the shoulders completely and concentrate on expanding the chest when doing these exercises.

Pushing in
Tense your pectorals and biceps and push your fingertips against each other without moving the arms. Do 20 times.

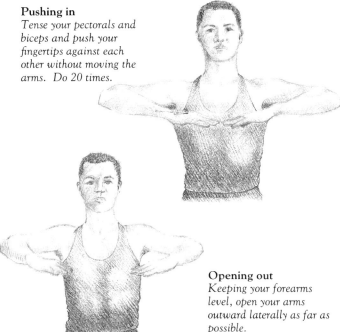

Opening out
Keeping your forearms level, open your arms outward laterally as far as possible.

Upward stretch

Tension in the shoulders and upper back builds up unconsciously and can be hard to identify until you begin moving and stretching the upper body. Stretching the sides of the body opens up the upper body helping to locate tension spots. It also relaxes and lengthens the muscles of the upper back and arms. Feel the relaxation and heaviness in the shoulders after each upward stretch. Think of pulling on a rope with alternate hands.

2 Stretch up as high as you can with your right arm, while pulling down with your left shoulder. Then reverse, stretching up with your left arm, in a slow rhythmic motion. Repeat the exercise 20 times.

1 Stand upright with your feet slightly apart and parallel. Distribute your weight evenly. Raise your arms straight above your head.

Abdominal muscles

The stomach responds rapidly to regular toning exercises. You can see the effects as your shape improves. As the abdomen becomes stronger your tummy will become tighter, the tissues less slack and flabby, while the abdominal muscles themselves will become more clearly defined. You will also put less strain on your back. Sit-ups provide a good abdominal exercise, but you should never practise them with completely straight legs especially if you have a slightly weak back or are generally unfit. It is best to do them on an empty stomach. Do not slump after each exercise.

Sit-ups

These provide the standard abdominal workout, tightening and strengthening the area between lower pelvis and stomach. Practise them with slightly bent knees and if you find your feet rise off the floor, wedge yourself underneath a sofa or bed or get a friend to hold them in place. Always begin slowly and gently if you are unfit and don't do any more sit-ups than you can manage without getting soreness or "burn".

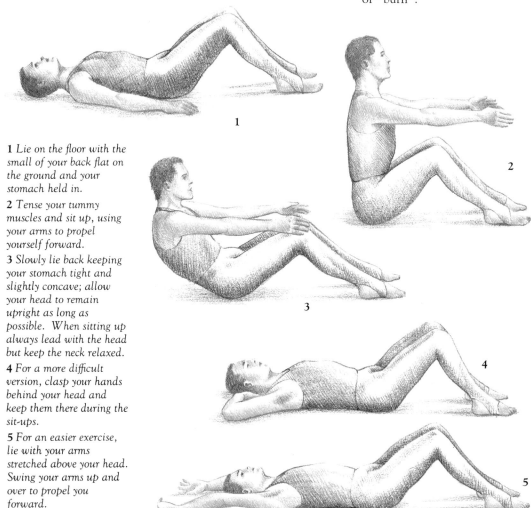

1 *Lie on the floor with the small of your back flat on the ground and your stomach held in.*

2 *Tense your tummy muscles and sit up, using your arms to propel yourself forward.*

3 *Slowly lie back keeping your stomach tight and slightly concave; allow your head to remain upright as long as possible. When sitting up always lead with the head but keep the neck relaxed.*

4 *For a more difficult version, clasp your hands behind your head and keep them there during the sit-ups.*

5 *For an easier exercise, lie with your arms stretched above your head. Swing your arms up and over to propel you forward.*

Abdominal exercises

This exercise tones the abdomen, helps to align and adjust the pelvis, and counteracts strain and tension in the lower lumbar region. Exercising this part of the body involves minimal, subtle movements so concentrate on feeling the change to a very specific area, just beneath the navel and around the pubic bone.

1 *Lie flat with your arms stretched out to the sides. Pull in your abdominal muscles tightly, keeping the base of your spine flat on the floor.*
2 *Tense your buttocks and let your pubic bone push up and forward. Relax for two seconds. Repeat ten times.*

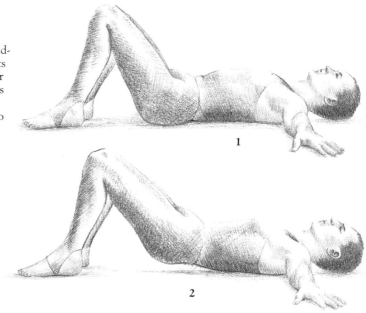

Sitting pelvic tilt

Seating problems account for the majority of postural faults, which develop either through laziness, tiredness, or using the wrong furniture. By becoming aware of how to sit correctly you can overcome bad habits. This exercise also encourages abdominal and pelvic fitness.

1 *Sit well forward on a chair with your back upright and feet together. Hold the chair back.*
2 *Tighten the abdominal and buttock muscles, allowing the pubic bone to jut slightly forward and up. Keep your chest stretched upright, your lower spine straight. Relax. Repeat ten times.*

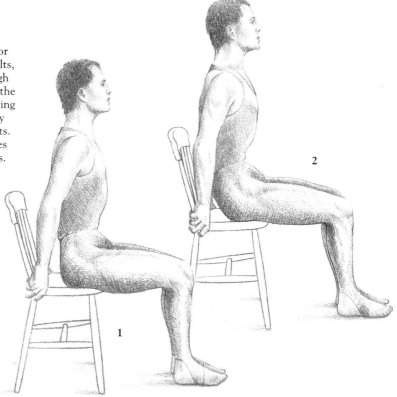

Back muscles

These exercises are designed to stretch the back muscles and those along the sides of the body. Do them very slowly and rhythmically to obtain a maximum stretch, creating a sensation of lengthening your upper body from the hip joints, buttocks, and upper thighs all the way along your body to the arm sockets. You can exercise the long back muscles safely lying down to avoid strain–use a pillow to support your hips if you have a weak lower back. The arching exercise will also stretch the muscles between the shoulderblades, the backs of the upper arms, the buttocks, and the backs of the thighs.

Backarch

Whenever practising back exercises that involve lying stretched out on the floor, concentrate on extending the spine and limbs to their fullest in order to counteract the shortening of the back muscles and prevent strain. You should also avoid hunching the shoulders, neck strain, and shortening of the neck muscles.

1 Lie on your tummy as below.
2 Clench your buttocks and raise your legs and trunk, pulling back your arms. Hold for five seconds then relax. Repeat five times.

Backstretch

By extending your legs and arms simultaneously while lying on the floor on your tummy you will be giving the back muscles, legs, hips and sides of your body a uniform stretch that helps to improve all-over posture and strengthen the back. Keep your neck relaxed and fully extended and your head in alignment with your neck.

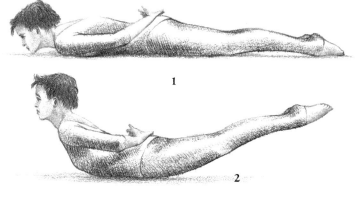

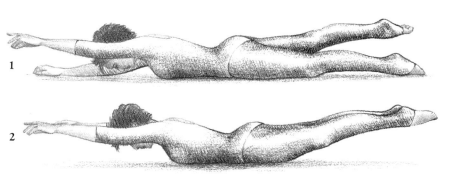

1 Lie flat on your front and make sure your back is not arched. Raise your left arm and right leg,   *pulling back and forward in opposing directions.*   *2 Repeat with the other arm and leg. Then do the exercise with both arms and legs simultaneously.*   *Relax. Do the whole sequence five times.*

Leglift

Do not attempt this exercise if you have a lower spine injury. Using a pillow to support the hips takes the strain off the lumbar region and encourages the body to adopt the correct posture automatically. At first; do not lift the legs too high.

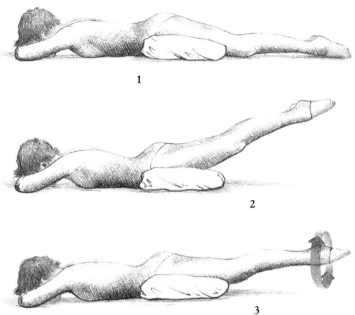

1

2

1 *Supporting your hips with a small cushion, lie down on your tummy. Rest your forehead in your clasped hands.*

2 *Slowly lift both legs off the floor by clenching the thigh and buttock muscles.*

3 *Hold for a few seconds then lower slowly. Repeat ten times.*

3

Forward stretch

This exercise stretches and tones the entire back, the hips, and the backs of the legs. Begin by keeping your feet pointed, to prevent straining the achilles and hamstring tendons. Then gradually try to flex both feet. Never arch the small of the back when sitting up. Tensing your tummy muscles very tightly should prevent you from hollowing the spine.

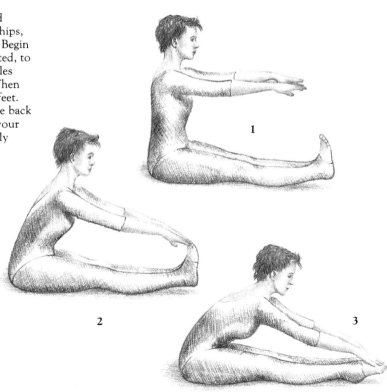

1

1 *Sit upright, with your legs stretched out on the floor. Hold your arms out in front.*

2 *With your feet pointed, slowly stretch your upper body over your legs, gripping your feet with your hands.*

3 *Do the same with your feet flexed. Repeat each ten times.*

2

3

Pelvis

Pelvic tone and placing not only contribute to the
health of the inner, reproductive organs but also help
to guard against lower backache by relieving the
amount of strain which may accumulate in the lower
lumbar region. Taut, toned abdominal muscles also
help to hold the pelvis in correct alignment, preventing
the weakness and slouching that leads to postural
problems. These exercises, which concentrate on improving pelvic alignment, also help to tone the lower
back, hips, and abdomen. They will help counteract
the effects of menstrual aches and cramps, faulty posture, and other problems that affect the health and well-
being of the pelvic region.

Forward pelvic tilt

Apart from relieving cramp,
strain, and congestion in the
pelvic tissues and internal
organs, pelvic exercises can also
adjust sloppy, unbalanced posture where it affects the lower
back and hips. This is very
common if you stand a lot,
when you get tired, and during
pregnancy and menstruation.
Remember when tilting and ad-
justing the pelvis always to pull
the upper body up as fully as
possible to exert a counter-
stretch. This will help you to
isolate the pelvic area.

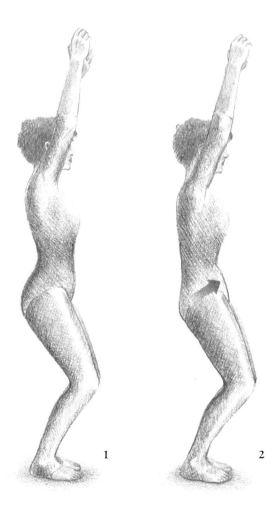

*1 Stand feet slightly apart
and parallel, stretch your
arms up and bend your
knees slightly.*
*2 Rhythmically roll the
pelvis forward. As you
relax the pelvis, keep your
abdominal muscles taut,
with your upper body
stretched upward
throughout. Don't arch
your back. Repeat twenty
times.*

Forward drop

This exercise will help you to adjust overall posture and place the pelvis correctly by uncurling the entire spine and hips from a fully relaxed and concave position. To check the standing position you should aim for, hang a tape measure down the centre of a full-length mirror. If you stand sideways this should run from the top of your head, through the earlobe, shoulder, the middle of the waist, the centre of the hip joint, behind the kneecap and in front of the ankle bone. Check that the upper body is pulled up the from the ribcage and abdominals, the tummy is held in, the pelvis tucked slightly forward, the lower spine flat, the buttocks and seat held under the head, and the neck and shoulders relaxed.

2 *Drop your head and arms and begin to roll your upper body over onto your knees. Let your body hang relaxed.*

1 *Keep your feet parallel and slightly apart and relax your knees. Raise your arms above your head.*

3 *Now begin to rise, keeping a curved back, and unrolling the upper body very slowly.*

Alternate pulls

Stretching the body while lying fully relaxed on the floor ensures that you feel every limb and muscle group as you extend it. It also helps to increase your awareness of the abdomen as your centre of strength. When stretching your legs and arms concentrate on keeping your lower back firmly pressed to the floor. Hold in your tummy and pull the ribcage up. But don't allow it to jut out.

"Shorten" one leg while stretching the opposite arm. Relax and reverse.

Legs, ankles, and feet

Balance and agility are essential prerequisites for good
posture and fitness. These qualities depend on the
flexibility of the toes, ankles, knee and hip joints and
on the strength in the arches of the feet. The muscles
and tendons that run from the lower back along the
legs to the feet should also be flexible. The leg joints
and hips are the first areas to stiffen up through inactivity, and the weaker your leg muscles, the stiffer your
knees, hips, or ankles. Running, skipping, or fast walking can help to tone the legs while swimming flexes the
thighs and hips. But specific bending and stretching
exercises for the feet and legs are most effective of all.

Knee bends

Dancers do pliés, or knee
bends, to strengthen the legs,
knees, and ankles. Turn out the
legs as much as possible from
the hips, and pull in the buttocks to extend the leg muscles
fully. You can gain extra
stretch and strengthen the
arches of the feet by taking your
heels off the ground.

First position
*1 Face a bar or chair back
and hold on with both
hands. Place your feet in
the first ballet position
with the heels together,
and the feet and legs
turned out.*

*2 Bend your knees, first
halfway; then fully,
allowing your heels to rise
off the ground.*

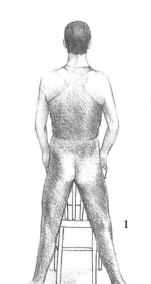

Second position
*1 Take up the second
ballet positon, with your
legs 2 ft (60 cm) apart.*
*2 Bend your knees, this
time keeping your feet flat
on the ground. Feel the
stretch in your hips, groin,
and inner thigh.*

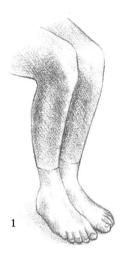

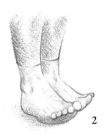

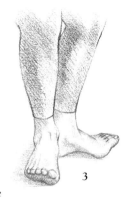

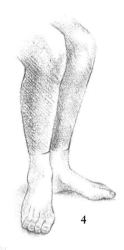

1 *Sit on a chair and place your feet together.*
2 *Raise them until only the heels rest on the ground.*
3 *Lift them out into an open position.*

Ankles and feet

This exercise will help improve the mobility and flexibility of your feet. It may prove difficult to do at first, but as your feet become more flexible it should get easier. Always do foot exercises barefoot.

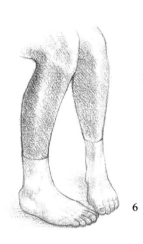

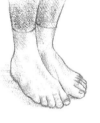

4 *Lower your toes.*
5 *Slide your feet together.*
6 *Reverse the exercise, with your toes turned in and touching, and the weight on the balls of your feet. Slide your feet back to the starting position.*

Foot grips

The toes and the tiny muscles that support the foot's arch need as much flexing and exercising as any other part of the foot. Simply wriggling the toes and opening and closing them to make a fan shape helps to relieve cramp and overcome the restrictive effects of wearing tight shoes and stockings. Tightly gripping the toes and hollowing the arch or picking something up with the toes also improves flexibility.

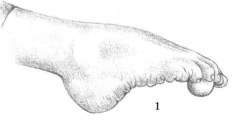

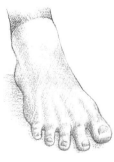

1 *Pick up a small soft ball (or a pencil) with your toes.*
2 *Open your toes to make a fan shape.*

Breathing

Oxygen is the basic stuff of life. Each cell of the body relies on it for fuel. Most of the time we are not conscious of the fact that we are breathing, yet during a single day we take between 16,000 and 23,000 breaths. Each breath uses up about 250 mls of oxygen and disposes of about 200 mls of carbon dioxide. For us to feel relaxed and well, the balance of these two substances is all-important. Under normal circumstances we cannot regulate the amount of oxygen in the air we breathe. But we can regulate the levels of oxygen and carbon dioxide within the body by changing the way we breathe.

Normally, our breathing is controlled by the parts of the brain that monitor the ratio of oxygen and carbon dioxide in the body–we exhale as soon as the level of carbon dioxide in the blood makes it more acid. Fast or very deep breathing (known as hyperventilation or over-breathing) causes the body to eliminate too much carbon dioxide. This may make the blood too alkaline, producing unpleasant side-effects such as dizziness by cutting off supplies of carbon dioxide to the brain. Forced, unnatural styles and rhythms of breathing can therefore upset the finely tuned feedback mechanism that controls our oxygen intake and carbon dioxide output. Shallow, irregular breathing, which can be caused by illnesses involving the respiratory tract, faulty posture, or physical tension, also upsets the balance.

But you can control the way you breathe. In order to fill your lungs evenly with air, you need to breathe rhythmically from the diaphragm, the dome-like muscle between the chest and the abdominal cavity. This also pulls the air down into the lower lungs, where most of the blood circulates. There are several exercises that you can do to help you control your breathing and they are all based on diaphragmatic breathing. Some are dynamic, helping you to release tension, others have more of a tranquillizing effect. All are useful aids to relaxation. In addition to the exercises shown in this chapter, yoga (see pages 133-45) and some forms of meditation (see pages 147-53) also incorporate breathing techniques. In the long term, increasing the amount of exercise you take will also increase your lung capacity and help with the quality of your breathing.

Posture also influences the way we breathe. If you slouch, or your chest and rib cage are slumped and concave, the diaphragm is immobilized and breathing is confined mainly to the upper chest area. Chest breathing puts strain on the heart as it must pump through more blood to carry the same amount of oxygen. It can also lead to increased blood pressure as the blood circulates more rapidly. Quick upper chest breathing generally produces cramped, shallow respiration which only fills about one quarter of the lung's capacity.

Whenever you are relaxing, try to regulate, quieten, or centre your breathing. You should do this especially when you are out of doors, whether walking or sitting in the garden or lying on a beach. Inhaling fresh, unpolluted air (especially by the sea, in the countryside, or at high altitudes), helps to refresh and clarify the mind and bring fresh supplies of oxygen-rich blood to all the tissues of your body.

Hyperventilation

Stress-related illnesses and anxiety attacks are frequently associated with hyperventilation. Often there is a
vicious circle of cause and effect, with faulty breathing
producing symptoms of anxiety, which then make the
breathing worse. Habitual hyperventilation is linked
with many unpleasant symptoms–dizziness, fainting,
sweating, numbness, palpitations, and chest pain.
These all occur as a result of depleted supplies of carbon dioxide in the body.

Of course, most of us breathe incorrectly only some
of the time, usually at times of stress and tension, so
these symptoms may not appear. But warning signals
that you may be overbreathing include frequent yawn-
ing, gulping, sighing, holding your breath, and visibly
moving the upper chest, throat, and shoulders while
you are talking and breathing.

Some personality types and professions are particularly linked to breathing problems. The people
most prone to hyperventilation tend to be hard-working, stressed, "type A" personalities or compulsive perfectionists. Athletes, actors, singers, and musicians
who play brass or woodwind instruments also find
overbreathing to be a problem. Dr Claude Lum, a
noted researcher in this field, has shown that hyperventilation also becomes more pronounced at certain
times: during social gatherings and parties, on aircraft,
over weekends or holidays when the "workaholic" has
to slow down, and as a result or drinking alcohol.

You can do a simple test to find out whether you are
overbreathing or whether you breathe naturally from
the diaphragm. Put one hand on the upper part of
your chest and the other on the lower edge of your rib-
cage, where the abdomen begins. If the lower edge of
the rib-cage expands and the stomach rises first at the
start of each breath, then you are using your diaphragm
correctly. If only your chest moves, you are breathing
inefficiently.

Often, correcting the breathing problem will also put
right the associated disorder. Doctors at London's St
Bartholomew's Hospital have found that teaching
agoraphobics how to breathe correctly and overcome
their panic and anxiety symptoms provides a lasting
and successful relief from the condition.

*Test your use of your
diaphragm by putting your
hands in this position. At
the start of each breath
your stomach should rise
and the lower edge of your
rib-cage should expand.*

Breathing exercises

Many of us breathe incorrectly at times of stress and tension. Bursts of rapid breathing accompanied by shortness of breath or tightness of the chest and throat are a familiar part of the fight or flight response. Conscious relaxation and breathing exercises can be very helpful, although if you are going through an anxious period and are worried about your breathing, you should avoid exercises that might confuse you. Begin by trying to breathe slowly and emphasize the out-breath to help restore your breathing to normal. The exercises in this chapter can help you overcome different types of stress from mental anxiety to physical strain. When doing them, relax as fully as possible and concentrate completely on your breathing. Never force your breath and stop if you begin to feel dizzy. After you have finished, try to remain aware of how it feels to breathe smoothly and rhythmically.

1 Holding your right nostril shut with the edge of your right thumb, inhale to a count of eight through the left nostril. Then place your index finger against your left nostril and hold your breath for a further count of eight.

Breath control
You can overcome shallow, irregular breathing by practising breath control. While breathing rhythmically, concentrate on raising your abdomen as you inhale and consciously fill your lower, mid, and upper lungs with air. As you hold your breath be aware of the expansion of the ribs at the front and back of your body–the sensation should be like steadily blowing up a balloon. When exhaling, press in the diaphragm like a set of bellows, drawing it in toward the spine. Ensure that you empty your lungs completely before inhaling again. Stop if you feel dizzy or faint, or if you begin to gulp in too much air.

2 Release your thumb from the right nostril and exhale to a count of eight, keeping your index finger on the left nostril. Then begin inhaling again through the right nostril, reversing the sequence. Repeat the two rounds five times.

Dynamic breathing exercise

Emphasizing the out-breath is one very effective way of discharging tension and helping to clear mental stress. Exhale audibly and dynamically–use the sounds "shoo" or "hoo" and extend them for as long as possible. This will ensure that you expel all the air in your lungs before expanding and filling them again, helping to exercise the lungs. Relaxing the upper body and dropping it forward as you exhale compresses the chest cavity and makes you more aware of the need to expand your lungs fully as you breathe in again. Concentrate on exhaling fully as you lower your body and relax for a couple of seconds before inhaling and coming up again.

1 *Stand upright, with your feet slightly apart and breathe in through the nose to a count of four until your lungs are fully expanded.*

3 *When you are completely relaxed, slowly rise again, inhaling to a steady count of eight. When you are upight, exhale to a count of two and begin the exercise again.*

2 *Sharply expel the air through your mouth with a hissing or shooing sound as you drop your upper body toward the floor, bending your knees.*

Tranquillizing exercise

This exercise is derived from yoga. It takes a little time to co-ordinate, but is well worth the effort. It will clear your head if you are tired and overworked, while at night, it can help to encourage sleep. Do not force inhalation and exhalation. Ideally, you should inhale, hold, and exhale each time to a steady count of eight. But at first you may have to limit this to four, gradually increasing the count.

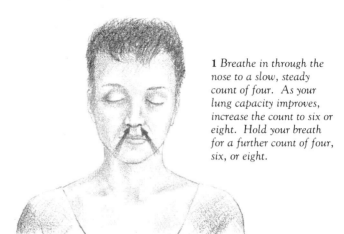

1 Breathe in through the nose to a slow, steady count of four. As your lung capacity improves, increase the count to six or eight. Hold your breath for a further count of four, six, or eight.

2 Without moving your body, begin to breathe out to a slow, steady count of four, six, or eight. Expel all the air completely. After the last number, begin again.

Breathing positions

Bad posture can hinder the free flow of air in and out of the body. To ensure that your body is fully relaxed and the lungs and diaphragm are free to move, lie down in this position (right). It will take the strain off the lower back, neck, and shoulders, relieve strain on the internal organs, and encourage a more relaxed pattern of breathing. This will gradually become easier, and you will eventually be able to adopt the pattern whatever you are doing.

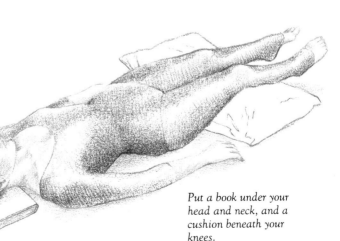

Put a book under your head and neck, and a cushion beneath your knees.

Yoga

Yoga is a philosophy of living that had its genesis many thousands of years ago in India. It survives today the world over as the oldest and most holistic system of mind-body fitness. Literally translated, yoga means union, and it aims to unite physical, mental, and spiritual health. It induces spiritual awareness, deep relaxation, mental tranquillity, concentration and clarity, fused with physical strength and suppleness.

But in order to obtain this mind/body harmony and inner calm it is not necessary to delve very deeply into the yogic philosophy–or to be a contortionist. You can take up yoga at any age and level of fitness. The postures (which are known as "asanas") can be adapted to allow for physical injury or weakness. Go to a yoga class if you are unsure which positions to attempt. Unlike more vigorous exercise systems, the asanas are practised slowly, without pushing or jerking the body, so there is no risk of strain or injury.

Yoga is unique because it not only stretches all parts of the body, it also massages the internal organs and glands. And its co-ordinated system of breathing relaxes mind and body, stimulates the circulation, and increases the supply of oxygen to all the tissues. The parts of the body which yoga stretches and tones most dramatically are the back, the stomach, the chest, and the lungs. The result is that the stiffening-up processes due to inactivity, tiredness, incorrect posture, and ageing are reversed.

Regular practise of the sequence of asanas illustrated in this chapter will give you an introduction to the basics of yoga, providing a framework for assessing your individual capabilities, and a basis for improving all-round flexibility and fitness.

There is much to be gained from following this basic session of yoga to promote your general health, and from concentrating on individual poses to help with particular health problems. If you are going to do yoga seriously and practise regularly to obtain maximum health and fitness benefits you should train with a teacher. You will learn a fuller repertoire of breathing exercises and asanas and perhaps even meditation techniques.

When practising yoga it is important to follow a sequence of asanas that has been structured carefully–you should not select one or two individual asanas and hope them to be beneficial. This is because the stretches of one position are balanced by counterstretches in the next. You should also start with preliminary exercises to limber up the body for the more strenuous asanas–in this book, the sun salutation performs this role. So if you do not want to follow the basic session in this chapter, you should seek the guidance of a qualified yoga teacher in adopting the best sequence for your particular needs.

Whichever direction you decide to follow, you should set aside at least three times a week to practise regularly. Do not skip on the relaxation periods that precede and follow each yoga session. Relaxation–of both body and mind–is vital to yoga, making it a good way of banishing tension. So these are valuable and intrinsic elements of yoga and they are necessary if you are to achieve a true and harmonious balance of physical and mental well-being.

A basic session

This sequence of asanas is designed to suit both beginners and more advanced students of yoga. It includes the fundamental postures that form the core of all yoga practice. These postures encourage suppleness of the spine and joints and muscular tone. They also tone the internal organs. Perform the asanas slowly, with grace and control. Hold each final position for as long as you can to obtain the fullest possible stretch. Slow, deep, abdominal breathing and a calm, focused mind will help to relax you, encouraging confidence and a sense of mind-body harmony. The asanas in this sequence are combined in a specific order to complement and counterbalance the effects of one another, with the result that they stretch and tone all parts of the body fully and equally.

Preliminaries

Practise every day or every other day, at the same time if possible. Set aside a time that is free from interruptions and do not rush through the sequence. For maximum comfort wear loose clothing and use a practise mat or blanket on which to perform the asanas. Begin and end the session by relaxing in the corpse pose.

The sequence of asanas

Start your basic session with a few minutes' rest in the **corpse pose,** then slowly stand up to do the **sun salutation.** Do its twelve positions slowly. Link them gracefully and rhythmically, with each movement flowing into the next. The bending and stretching movements warm up and flex the entire body in preparation for the asanas.

The **headstand** is the first asana in the sequence. Use confidence and patience to master this pose. Once perfected, it will bring great physical and mental benefits. Next come two asanas that are deeply relaxing and invigorating: the **shoulderstand** and the **plough.** Holding both for as long as possible ensures that you will obtain a full stretch of the upper spine and neck. Keep your back and legs straight when your body is inverted in the shoulderstand, pulling the legs and hips back as far as possible in the plough.

The **fish,** performed next, counterstretches the body after the three preceding asanas. It compresses the neck and upper spine, extends the chest and ribcage, and helps relieve stiffness of the upper back. Next come the **head to knee pose** and the forward bend, which provides an extended back stretch, emphasizing the base of the spine and the muscles along the backs of the legs. Do not treat this merely as a toe-touching exercise. Extend your body

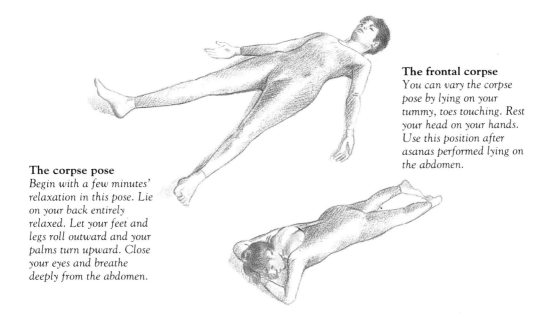

The frontal corpse
*You can vary the corpse
pose by lying on your
tummy, toes touching. Rest
your head on your hands.
Use this position after
asanas performed lying on
the abdomen.*

The corpse pose
*Begin with a few minutes'
relaxation in this pose. Lie
on your back entirely
relaxed. Let your feet and
legs roll outward and your
palms turn upward. Close
your eyes and breathe
deeply from the abdomen.*

slowly and hold the pose as long as you can, stretching and flattening the body on to the knees. Move gently, without straining.

The next two asanas, the **cobra** and the **bow**, provide a counterpull to the forward bend and the plough. They arch and flex the entire back, expanding the chest, stretching the neck, and toning the abdominal area.

Having practised a series of asanas that provide both a forward and a backward stretch to the back, you now sit up for the **half spinal twist**. This rotates the upper body, twisting the spine laterally to relieve strain and tension in the back, hips, and neck. Keep your body erect, your shoulders level, and your tummy pulled in.

You now stand up slowly and take your position for the **triangle**, the last asana in this basic session. It extends the movement of the half spinal twist, tones the digestive organs and spinal nerves, and stretches the spine laterally. Make sure that you bend over slowly and smoothly without jerking. Take a few slow, full breaths in the final position before relaxing and repeating it on the other side.

Finish in the **corpse pose**, which you should also use between asanas, to give extra concentraion and relaxation. Make your final corpse pose more complete than the one at the beginning–the asanas will have stretched your muscles.

The sun salutation

The sun salutation (or surya namaskar) consists of twelve exercises that warm and limber up the body in preparation for the asanas. The sequence of movements should be smoothly linked together and co-ordinated to make a complete whole. Every position stretches the body in a way different from the previous one, while the sequence alternately expands and contracts the chest to encourage smooth and rhythmic breathing. Performed each day it will encourage suppleness and strength of the spine and joints. One round of the sun salutation consists of two sequences: the first leads with the right foot in positions 4 and 9, the second leads with the left. Begin by practising four rounds, and gradually increase this to twelve.

1 *Stand upright, knees and feet together, legs straight, palms touching. Distribute your weight evenly and exhale.*

2 *Inhaling, raise arms above head, arching back from the waist, and pushing the pelvis out.*

3 *Exhaling, bring your upper body forward, pressing head and chest against knees with your hands on the floor. Bend knees if necessary.*

4 *Inhaling, extend one leg back, sinking into a deep lunge, one knee on the ground. Arch back, lift chin, and look up.*

5 *Holding your breath, draw the supporting leg back, your weight supported on hands and toes. Keep head and spine in line and look down.*

6 *Exhaling, lower in stages your knees, chest, and forehead; keep the hips tucked up and the toes curled under.*

12 *Exhaling slowly, return to an upright relaxed position, resting your arms at the sides of your body. Make sure your weight is evenly distributed and your body relaxed. Repeat the sequence, leading with the other leg.*

11 *Inhaling, extend your arms forward then up and back over your head. Arch back slowly, as in position 2.*

10 *Exhaling, draw the other leg forward and bend your body from the waist, mirroring position 3.*

9 *Inhaling, step forward, with one foot between your hands, in a mirror image of position 4.*

7 *Inhaling, lower your hips to the ground, point your toes, and arch back keeping your legs together, relaxing shoulders. Tilt your head up and back.*

8 *Exhaling, tuck your toes under, and lift your hips so the body assumes an inverted V shape. Press heels down, drop head and push shoulders back.*

The headstand

The headstand (or sirshasana) has so many benefits that it is sometimes called the king of asanas. By stimulating the flow of oxygen and blood to the brain it improves memory and concentration, and sharpens the sensory faculties. By reversing the normal gravitational pull, it rests the heart, improves circulation and relieves strain on the lower back. But you should never do the headstand if you suffer from any of these disorders: very high or low blood pressure, heart disease, severe sinus or catarrh problems, eye disorders, or thyroid dysfunction. When first attempting the pose, ask someone to help you keep your balance. Stop at point 5 or 6 if you cannot do the complete headstand.

1 *Kneel down, put your weight on your forearms, and clasp your hands around your elbows.*

2 *Unclasp hands, placing them in front of you, fingers interlocked.*

3 *Put the crown of your head in the cradle made by your hands, the top of your head resting on the ground.*

4 *Gradually straighten your knees and raise your hips.*

5 *Keeping your knees straight, walk your feet in as close to your head as possible. Keep your neck in line with your spine by pulling your hips back.*

6 *Bend your knees into your chest; raise your feet off the ground, projecting your hips back. Rest for a few minutes.*

7 *Keeping your knees bent, propel them slowly upward using your tummy muscles.*

8 *Very slowly straighten your legs, putting your weight onto your forearms.*

Come down by reversing steps 5, 6, and 7. Rest in the child's pose.

The shoulderstand

In Sanskrit the shoulderstand is called sarvangasana, which literally means "all parts pose". It stretches the neck and upper back while stimulating the thyroid and parathyroid glands. Rather than repeating it, try to hold the pose, resting in the position and breathing deeply for anything from 30 seconds to 5 minutes. Come out of the shoulderstand by lowering the legs to a 40-degree angle, placing your palms down behind you and rolling your back down, vertebra by vertebra, until it is flat on the floor. Then slowly lower your legs.

1 *Lie on the floor with your feet together and your hands at your sides, palms down. Inhale and raise both legs slowly, pressing down with your hands onto the floor.*
2 *Lift your hips, bringing your legs over your head at a 45° angle.*

1

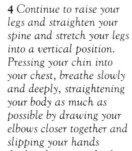

2

3 *Bend your arms and put hands on hips to support your lower body. Support the front of your body with your thumbs and hold your fingers across your back.*

3

The child's pose

This relaxation pose regulates the flow of blood after the headstand. It also disimpacts the spine and stretches out the back muscles. Kneel on the ground and place your buttocks on your feet with the heels pointing out. Rest your forehead on the floor and place your arms at sides of your body, palms turned up.

4 *Continue to raise your legs and straighten your spine and stretch your legs into a vertical position. Pressing your chin into your chest, breathe slowly and deeply, straightening your body as much as possible by drawing your elbows closer together and slipping your hands further down your back.*

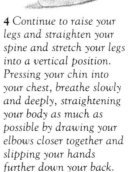

4

The plough

The plough (or halasana) is really an extension of the shoulderstand and gives the maximum possible stretch to the entire length of the spine. It also flexes and strengthens the back, shoulder, and arm muscles, and massages the internal organs. If you cannot fully reach the floor with your feet, put a cushion under your feet. The pull of your legs will gradually stretch and flex your spine. Use the shoulderstand roll-out to come out of the plough.

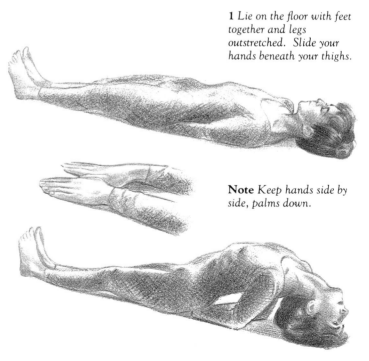

1 Lie on the floor with your feet together, your hands at your sides, palms down. Inhale, and lift both legs vertically, then exhale and raise your hips off the floor.

3 With your toes tucked under, walk your feet slowly as far behind your head as possible, pushing your torso up, keeping heels back. Clasp your hands, and stretch your arms out behind your back.

2 Supporting your lower back with your hands, exhale and tip your legs overhead. If your feet cannot reach the floor, stay in this position.

1 Lie on the floor with feet together and legs outstretched. Slide your hands beneath your thighs.

The fish

The fish (or matsyasana) should follow the plough and shoulderstand. It provides a counter-stretch to relieve tension across the back and counteract stiffness in the neck and shoulders. The pose will strengthen the small of the back, exercise the chest, and improve breathing and lung capacity. Stay in the pose for about half the time you spent in the plough.

Note *Keep hands side by side, palms down.*

2 Pressing on your elbows, and flattening your forearms against the floor, inhale and arch back. Rest the crown of your head on the floor.

The head to knee pose

The janu sirasana uses the bent leg to stretch the hips and groin muscles while the weight of the torso in turn stretches the straight leg and flexes the hamstrings. The forward stretch compresses the abdomen and massages the internal organs. It also gives a stretch to the spine and back muscles. Bend over slowly and obtain the full stretch gradually as you become more supple.

1 Sit upright with legs outstretched. Bend one leg and bring the foot in until the sole touches the top of the other thigh. Stretch arms up and inhale.

2 Exhale and stretch forward from the base of your spine. Clasp your foot, pressing your body along your leg as far as possible. Breathe deeply, then relax. Repeat on the other side.

Forward bend

The paschimothanasana provides the spine and backs of the legs with a full and extended stretch, while strengthening the abdominal muscles and toning the internal organs. Avoid curving the spine and hunching the shoulders. Concentrate on keeping the knees straight and bringing the torso well forward. Don't aim your head at your knees. Never push or force, but ease yourself forward gradually. Exhale and inhale slowly, and come up and down a few times before finally holding the pose.

1 From a lying position with arms stretched above your head sit up, inhaling. Flex your feet and clench your buttock muscles so you sit on the pelvic bone. Stretch your arms above your head and elongate your spine.

2 Pull in your abdominal muscles, exhale, and stretch forward from the pelvis, keeping your back straight. Let your chin reach toward your shins, your chest toward your thighs.

3 Continue stretching, keeping your legs straight and trying to flatten your upper body. Clasp your index fingers around your big toes.

The cobra

The cobra (or bhujangasana)
gives a strong backward stretch.
It expands the chest area,
strengthens the lower back, and
stimulates the adrenal glands.
Do not attempt the cobra if you
suffer from an over-active
thyroid. Visualize the slow,
sinuous, uncurling movements
of a snake, as you extend your
spine. Remember to relax the
shoulders and face and do not
force the stretch if your spine is
stiff. As you become more supple you will be able to increase
the backward curve of the
spine.

*1 Lie with your legs
together, your hands palms
down under your
shoulders, and your
forehead resting on floor.*

*2 Inhale, raising your
head, chest, and shoulders
off the floor. Straighten
your elbows and arch the
spine. Hold then relax
slowly. Don't push with
your arms.*

*3 Inhale, raise your torso
again, but come further up
and back so that your back
bends from the base of
your spine to neck.*

The bow

The bow (or dhanurasana)
should be performed as an extension of the cobra and involves raising both the upper
and lower body simultaneously
to stretch and strengthen the
back muscles and flex the spine.
The bow also tones the liver
and bowels, and reduces tension
and menstrual cramp. Once
you have mastered the bow, you
can increase these benefits by
rocking gently back and forward
on your abdomen. Beginners
will find it easier to do this with
legs lifted slightly apart.

*1 Lie flat with your head
down. Inhale and bend
your knees up, then grasp
your ankles and exhale.*

*2 Inhaling, lift your head
and chest while pulling on
your ankles, to raise your
trunk and thighs off the
floor. Hold for 3 breaths
then relax.*

The half spinal twist

The half spinal twist (or ardha matsyendrasana) rotates the spine, stretching it laterally to give the back greater flexibility and freedom of movement. It also tones the spinal nerves and liver and stimulates the adrenal glands. Hold your spine as upright as possible, keeping your shoulders level and breathing steadily. And try to twist around further each time you breathe out and hold the position, keeping your head up and eyes level for a few breaths, before repeating the position on the other side.

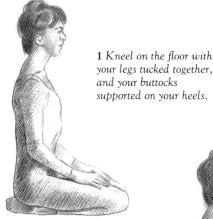

1 *Kneel on the floor with your legs tucked together, and your buttocks supported on your heels.*

2 *Shift your body over to the right of your feet.*

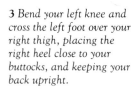

3 *Bend your left knee and cross the left foot over your right thigh, placing the right heel close to your buttocks, and keeping your back upright.*

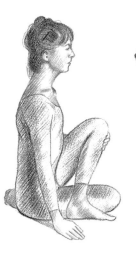

5 *Now grasp your left foot with your right hand. Exhale and twist around to the left as far as possible. Look over your left shoulder. Repeat on the other side.*

4 *Stretch your arms out sideways and twist your upper body to the left, keeping the weight evenly balanced on both buttocks.*

The triangle

Trikonasana, the triangle, is the
final posture in this basic yoga
session. It increases the benefits
of the half spinal twist, stretching the whole of the trunk,
especially the spine and the rib-
cage. It tones the abdomen,
increases lung capacity, and
improves overall balance. Keep
both knees straight and the hips
facing squarely forward. When
bending over to the side try to
avoid twisting the hips and keep
the ribs and chest expanded,
without allowing the upper
body to become concave.

*1 Stand with your feet
pointed slightly to the left
and about 3-4 ft (1 m)
apart. Stretch your left
arm out to the side and
your right arm up against
your right ear.*

*2 Exhaling, bend your
body over to the left.
Grasp your calf or ankle
with your left hand.
Repeat with the other side.*

The corpse pose

Every yoga session should begin
and end with a few minutes'
relaxation in the corpse pose.
Concentrate on breathing
deeply and rhythmically, and
try to empty your mind of
everything other than your
breathing, as if you were about
to meditate. At the end of the
session systematically relax each
part of the body, rotating the
legs, arms and spine in turn,
then stretching your limbs,
neck, and back. Feel the weight
of your body increase and allow
the pull of gravity to encompass
every inch of you as you sink
into the floor, your body deeply
and completely relaxed.

*Lie on your back in the
corpse pose at the end of
the session. If you do not
feel relaxed, try alternately
tensing and relaxing the
different parts of the body
(see page 113).*

Meditation

Meditation works by emptying the conscious mind. You direct your thoughts away from yourself and your problems, far from your work, family, environment, and relationships. As you do this you begin gradually to transcend the everyday level of consciousness, the hurly-burly of the here and now, and open up pathways to those parts of the brain that deal with unconscious thought and experience. When this happens, your arms or legs may begin to feel warm or heavy, and your head may begin to droop. In addition, your breathing will grow much shallower and slower as you become more and more relaxed, your mind increasingly divorced from your body and its immediate surroundings.

Meditation has been popular for over 2,500 years. Its chief appeal lies in its simplicity and in its undoubted benefits. It can quieten the surface "chatter" of the brain, exorcising extraneous, intrusive, and stressful thoughts. And it has the additional advantage that you can practise it on your own, without professional guidance, wherever you can find a congenial, undisturbed space. If you meditate regularly for about 20 minutes, once or twice a day, you can reduce your oxygen consumption and carbon-dioxide production by up to 20 per cent, lower your blood pressure, and reduce your level of blood lactate, a chemical produced in extra quantities at times of stress and anxiety. Biofeedback monitoring shows that meditation encourages the brain to produce an evenly balanced pattern of alpha and theta brainwave rhythms, indicating that the body is relaxed and the mind calm yet alert.

Regular meditation has helped people overcome addiction to tranquilizers and has reduced hypertension, insomnia, migraine, depression, anxiety, and other psychosomatic illnesses. It can also improve creativity, concentration, mental alertness, and memory, as well as stimulating physical energy.

Meditation relies on the close links between body and mind. When you meditate successfully, the alpha brainwaves that are produced show that you have reached the most balanced, relaxed, and harmonious state your body is able to attain. This freedom from physical tension and mental strain allows the body to switch to the "relaxation response", the complete opposite of the physical tension that occurs as a result of stress.

Recent research into the function of the human brain suggests that meditation expands brain function by encouraging a balance between the two separate hemispheres of the brain—the left-hand side, responsible for logical, rational, and scientific thought, and the creative, imaginative right-hand side. The healthiest, the most productive and fulfilled people are usually those in whom the activity of these two hemispheres is well-balanced.

For the purposes of controlling and surviving stress, and utilizing it creatively, this book concentrates on the therapeutic and relaxing benefits of meditation, rather than its deeper, more religious aspects. But whatever your attitude or goal in meditation, it will both improve your well-being and offer the added possibility of expanded creativity and enhanced sensory awareness.

Positions for meditation

The object of meditation is to produce harmony between mind and body. So adopting the right position is
important–you must feel relaxed without falling asleep
and the position you use must not make you twitch or
fidget or cause cramp or numbness.

There is no single "correct" position–the essential
thing is that it should be right for you. Lying on the
floor relaxes the back, limbs, and internal organs, and
supports the body. Sitting in a chair, with your back
supported, and your feet and legs together is a popular
pose. Sitting on the floor, legs outstretched with your
back propped up against the wall is also a good
position for many people. The full or half lotus
position, or simply sitting cross-legged, tailor fashion,
may appeal to anyone who is fit and active or who likes
to precede their meditation period with physical relaxation or conditioning exercises.

Sitting on a chair
*Use a hard or firm chair,
with your lower and mid
back supported, your feet
together, and your hands
resting lightly on your lap.
Try not to let your upper
body slouch.*

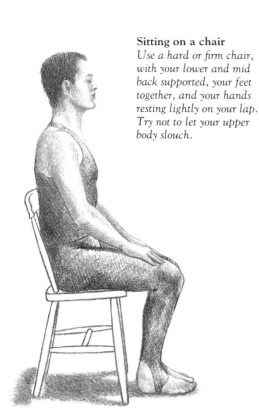

Cross-legged position
*Sit on the floor, keeping
your body upright and
your arms relaxed. Rest
your hands on your knees.*

Lotus position
Place both feet on opposite thighs to achieve the full lotus position, or one foot on the opposite thigh, the other foot tucked under the thigh, for a half lotus. Place your hands, palms open, on your knees.

Sitting on the floor
Sit on the floor with your legs outstretched and your knees and feet together. Hold your back straight against a wall and rest your hands on your thighs.

Lying down
Lie flat with your spine pressed flat along the floor. Keep your shoulders and neck completely relaxed.

Meditation techniques

To meditate successfully you will need peace and quiet. Find a tranquil, comfortable environment where you can be alone and undisturbed for 20 to 30 minutes. Harsh lighting, a room that is too cold or too hot, noise, and interruptions are all obstacles that can prevent you achieving the level of physical and mental quietness that is necessary for meditation. Some people find that incense, dim lights, or soft, repetitive background music help them meditate. Others find environmental sounds like birds singing, rain falling, or the sound of the ocean helpful in creating the right mood. But you may prefer complete silence and as little sensory stimulation as possible. Settle into a comfortable position that allows you to relax without falling asleep. Try to set aside about 20 to 30 minutes for meditation, remembering that there will be two stages—physical relaxation, followed by focusing and emptying the mind. When you begin meditating these initial stages may take time to attain. You must first relax—it is impossible to meditate if your body is tense.

Yogis use the Sanskrit syllable OM for meditation, letting their eyes wander over its curves.

Meditation and breathing
Breathing forms a pivot between conscious, voluntary states of being and transcendent, involuntary states of relaxation. Concentrating on your breathing is an ideal mental focusing device which helps block out other thoughts, blanking and quietening the mind by replacing mental clutter with a single object of contemplation. When you are relaxed, close your eyes, and begin to conentrate on the rhythm and feel of your breathing. This should be unforced and perhaps a little slower and shallower than usual. Imagine your tummy gently rising and falling with each in and out breath. For a while, think "in" as you breathe in through your nose, and as you breathe out through your nose or mouth think "out". Then start to count each breath, either repeating "one", or counting from one to ten. Concentrate on each breath, allowing yourself to be totally hypnotized by it; exclude all other thoughts from your mind. If you are counting, visualize the numbers each time you exhale by mentally "planting" them in the centre of your tummy. Don't anticipate or rush the next number—let each one melt gently into the next.

Meditating on an object

Instead of concentrating on your breathing, you may prefer to meditate by contemplating an object, for example a single perfectly formed flower, a mandala or eastern symbolic design, or a flickering candle. Silently repeating to yourself a single sound or using a special audio tape are effective methods for many people.

Forward de-stressing

This is a very powerful way of overcoming fear. You create a very detailed and complete picture in your mind of yourself in the potentially stressful situation. Then you feel and experience as fully as possible everything that could go wrong. You follow this by feeling and experiencing everything you know you have in your power to prevent the problem being stressful. This "positive programming" is far better than simply willing yourself to do better.

Visualization

You may prefer a more visual approach to meditation. Imagining yourself in idyllic surroundings, watching the wide expanse of a blue ocean or walking through a sun-dappled forest, may evoke deep mental and physical relaxation. One of the most powerful benefits of this type of meditation is its power, when incorporating certain specific techniques, to counteract negative thinking, nervousness, anxiety, fear, and low self-esteem. Special imaging techniques help to balance the left- and right-hand hemispheres of the brain, sharpen memory, and improve sensory awareness. They can also control our so-called involuntary physical actions. These techniques are used extensively as a part of numerous anti-stress and self-improvement systems such as silva mind control and sophrology. They are increasingly being used by doctors, dentists, athletes, pilots, artists, and teachers to defuse specifically stress-ful situations. In particular they can help overcome fear, apprehension, and nervousness. Apprehension–fear before the event–can be very stressful; and the use of positive imagery can help us to replace our negative thoughts and face pain, challenge, and difficult situations with new confidence. So positive imaging is increasingly used by psychologists as part of the treatment for phobias and anxiety states.

Using visualization
Lie or sit down and relax your body, breathing, and mind. Concentrate for a while on emptying your brain, focusing on the sound and rhythm of your breathing. Now imagine yourself lying or walking on a white, sandy beach. The sand is white and fine as talcum powder, tinged with pink. The sea is crystal clear, deep turquoise, or indigo blue, lapping at your feet. The breeze is gently caressing your body and hair. Feel the warm sun on your body, the sand between your toes, the sea spray on your face, the water lapping over your legs and arms. Then imagine you are lying in the sea, floating. Feel the buoyancy of the deep blue or tur-quoise salty water support your body effortlessly as you float on your back, your face upturned toward the sun. Feel your body become warm and heavy as the sun's rays spread their gentle warmth all around.

You can extend this type of meditation by imagining
yourself free of aches, pains, illness, infection, and
stress. See the part of your body that needs healing or
strengthening becoming strong and perfectly formed.
If you have an infection or inflammation think of your
white blood cells like fierce warriors or piranha fish att-
acking diseased unhealthy tissue and cells, destroying
them and encouraging new healthy cells to multiply in
their place. Imagine these warring cells carried along in
the lymph fluids which sweep up the diseased unhealthy cells, along with poisonous wastes, and flush
them out of your system for ever. At the same time
visualize fresh supplies of clean oxygen-rich blood
bathing and nourishing the healthy tissue and
strengthening it. If you have a migraine or tension
headache or tight aching muscles, think of the muscles
relaxing and lengthening; imagine your pulse rate and
blood pressure lowering, swollen throbbing dilated
blood vessels contracting, and the pain diminishing.

Left-right brain exercises

This type of exercise strengthens and expands brain
function by encouraging balance of the right- and left-
hand hemispheres of the brain. Practised regularly it
will help you to improve concentration and learning
skills, to solve problems and to overcome nervousness,
tension and stress.

Close your eyes and relax your body and breathing;
empty your mind. Keep your eyes closed. Now concentrate on one side of your brain and one eye.
Imagine with your right eye, and with the right side of
your brain, that you see a tree in spring covered in
pink and white blossoms. Now, using the left side of
the brain, and the left eye, see the same tree draped in
snow. Establish these two pictures clearly and dis-
tinctly and try and merge the images of the two trees
into the centre of your brain where they become one
tree covered in autumn foliage. You can devise further
exercises based on the other senses, e.g. taste (eating a
juicy apple and hot buttered toast), smell (smelling a
rose and a pot of coffee), and sound (classical music
and jazz) balancing and merging each on opposite sides
of the brain in a similar way.

Massage and acupressure

The relaxing, healing, and reviving powers of massage were recognized and recorded over 5,000 years ago. The therapeutic application of aromatic oils and unguents, and the practice of rubbing and pressing specific areas of the body to relieve pain and prevent illness were common among the civilizations of ancient Egypt, China, and Greece. Today the time-honoured techniques of massage, together with allied skills such as reflexology and acupressure, are again popular. More recent types of western massage, such as Swedish massage, are also widely used to relax and tone the body.

The aim of any massage system, eastern or western, is to ease away muscular tension, to dispel tiredness, and to reinforce depleted or unbalanced energy. Massage has the added benefit of helping you to prevent future physical weaknesses and strains. You can identify the prime tension spots, commonly found on the neck, shoulders, and back, by laying your hand flat onto your partner's body. Tense muscles feel rock hard, like tight, knotted cords. You may also detect hard, fibrositic nodules of tissue. Relaxed muscles, on the other hand, feel rather like putty, firm but flexible.

The various stroking, rubbing, kneading, pulling, and hacking movements used in massage will help to relax these tight and tense muscles. They will also improve circulation and encourage the elimination of toxic waste.

Eastern pressure-point techniques follow the same principles as acupuncture. According to acupuncture, the essential life force flows to all parts of the body through a system of meridians or energy lines. Acupressure and foot reflexology concentrate on balancing this flow of energy, by stimulating or sedating it. Pressure on the many acupuncture points all over the body can also strengthen or relax the internal organs, the spine, and the central nervous system. So these techniques are rather like acupuncture without needles, using thumb and finger pressure to treat the various points. Back pain, menstrual cramp, headaches, sleeplessness, fatigue, depression, and muscular tension all respond well to this type of treatment. Acupressure can also be used as a self-help technique to relieve the discomfort associated with sinus disorders, migraine, neuralgia, and other stress-related problems.

Aromatherapy is a branch of massage that involves rubbing therapeutic plant essences into the body. Absorbing the oils via the skin and inhaling their scent counteracts disharmony.

At their best, massage, acupressure, and reflexology are sharing experiences in which the sense of touch is heightened. During massage you become more aware of the most subtle feelings of pleasure and discomfort. So trust and empathy between the person giving and the person receiving the massage are essential if the receiver is to relax fully. The giver should warm and flex the hands before beginning and should never rush. The giver's movements should flow into each other imperceptibly, the hands remaining in perpetual contact with the receiver's body. In this chapter the most common tension spots have been selected for massage. You can treat these separately, but a whole-body massage (see p. 163) is best.

Giving a massage

Preparation is essential to create a mood conducive to mental relaxation and physical comfort. Work in a warm, ventilated room using soft, indirect lighting. A sensory background of soft music and fragrance may also help you create the right atmosphere. Scented candles, incense, or essential plant oils in a burner will permeate the air with fragrance and help create mental equilibrium. If possible, set aside as much as an hour for a full-body massage and make sure you won't be interrupted. When you are giving a massage, make sure that you are working at the right height so that you remain comfortable. If you get tired or tense you will transmit the sensation via jerky, taut, or awkward movements. When working on the floor, kneel down beside the blanket or mattress in order to be able to put your whole weight into the massage. When working standing up, use a massage table that is not too high or too low, so you do not strain your back.

Relaxation
Relax for a few minutes before a massage. Sit quietly, close your eyes, empty your mind, and concentrate on your breathing.

Beginning with the back

An area of prime sensitivity, the back is also prone to stiffness, aches, and pains. So devote the maximum time and attention to this part of the body. Begin by oiling and warming the back to encourage relaxation and establish initial contact with your partner. Use this first stage to familiarize yourself with your partner's body and its tension spots, and to gauge the correct rhythm and degree of pressure.

Oiling the back
Begin by placing your hands gently on your partner's upper back. Move them slowly down along the sides of the spinal column. As you reach the buttocks, separate your hands in a curving movement, pulling them slowly up the sides and along the shoulders. Repeat rhythmically until the entire back is oiled.

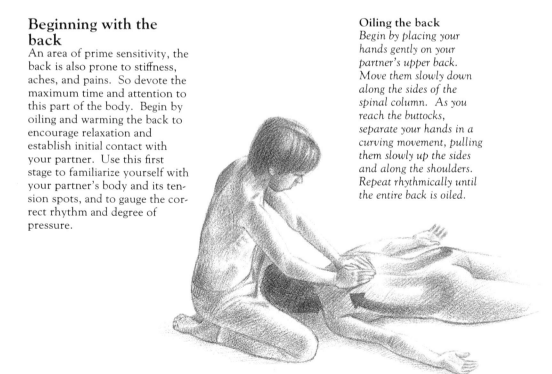

Massaging the back

Move over to the side of your partner's body and start to massage the different areas of the back more intensively. Concentrate on the areas of maximum strain and muscular tension such as the spine and the lower lumbar region. Thirty-one pairs of spinal nerves branch out over the back from the shoulders to the waist. These are connected to all the internal organs, while other, longer nerve branches radiate out to the limbs. Feel for areas of tension in the form of tight, knotted muscles and small granular nodules. End with a series of overall sweeping movements, like those used when oiling the back (see opposite).

1 The shoulderblade
Place one hand under your partner's shoulder. With the other hand, work in a deep, pressing, circular movement around the shoulderblade, using your fingers. Begin at the top of the shoulder and work down around the blade.

2 Circling the base of the spine
With alternate hands, work in a circular motion around the base of the spine, using a shallow, kneading movement. Keep the strokes broad to encompass the entire area.

4 Friction along the spine
Using both your thumbs, trace small, deep, rotating movements up either side of the spine, beginning at the base. Finish by pressing the thumbs briefly into the hollows at the base of the skull. Sweep your hands down and begin again.

3 "Rocking" stroke
Press one hand over the other and run both firmly up from the base of the spine to the neck. Then, using your index and middle fingers, press down the side of the spine, one hand following the other in a rocking motion.

Shoulders and neck

Strain or tension in the back
will automatically transmit itself
to the shoulders and neck
muscles. The muscles at the top
of the back merge with the neck
and support the head, so
shoulder and neck strain may
also result in headache and
eyestrain. Tense muscles can be
felt quite clearly and tough,
fibrous build-up may need deep,
prolonged squeezing and kneading to release tension. You can
massage the neck and shoulders
when your partner is lying
down, as an extension of the
back massage. Alternatively,
massage the neck and shoulders
in an upright position, where
you can feel more easily the
actual extent and location of the
strain and stiffness. Ensure that
your partner sits upright, with
head and neck completely
relaxed.

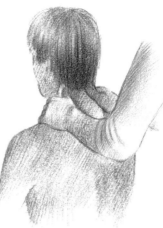

1 Kneading the neck
*Holding one shoulder to
prevent the upper body
from tipping over, grip the
flesh at the back of the
neck between your thumb
and forefinger and knead
firmly. Work up and
down from the base of the
skull to the shoulders.*

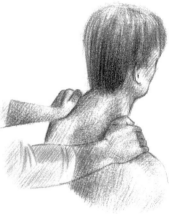

2 The shoulders
*Grip the top of the
shoulders and massage
deeply, from the base of
the neck to the outer edge.
Alternate small, deep,
rotating thumb strokes
with larger ones with the
heel of the hand.*

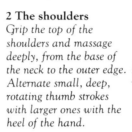

3 Deep shoulder stroke
*Use your thumbs to trace
deep lines out along the
shoulders from the base of
the neck. Stretch the
tissues as much as is
acceptable to the receiver.*

4 Turning the head
*Cup the chin and jaw in
one hand. Gently turn the
head using the other palm
on the crown of the head.
Repeat in other direction.
Do this only if your
partner's head is fully
relaxed.*

5 Massaging the nape
*Cup your partner's
forehead with one hand
and use the other to
massage the nape of the
neck near the base of the
skull. Use small, rotary
movements with your
thumbs and pinch the flesh
between thumb and fingers.*

The face

Massaging the face can ease away tiredness, facial tension, eyestrain, headaches, and sinus congestion. Strain is usually reflected in tightness in the jaw, forehead, and mouth. An expression that becomes rigidly set or false, etched with lines of worry or depression, is also a symptom of strain. When massaging the face ensure that your hands are clean; remove any surplus oil before touching the scalp and hair. Your movements should be firm, especially over the bony sinus areas on the cheekbones. Direct your strokes upward and outward, following the main lines of the facial expression. Do not pull, drag, squeeze, or pinch the facial skin, especially around the eyes; and do not work directly on the eyelids. The best subject position for a facial massage is lying down, to relieve the pull of gravity on the tissues.

1 Forehead

Place your fingers on your partner's temples and your thumbs at the centre of the forehead just above the brows. Moving up a fraction at a time, draw your thumbs apart slowly while exerting firm pressure. Work your way right up to the hairline.

3 Chin

Continue the horizontal stroking movements, this time working from the centre of the chin and separating your fingers to follow the curve of the jawline up to the earlobes.

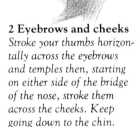

2 Eyebrows and cheeks

Stroke your thumbs horizontally across the eyebrows and temples then, starting on either side of the bridge of the nose, stroke them across the cheeks. Keep going down to the chin.

4 Cheeks and jaw

After stroking the tips of your fingers lightly down your partner's face, mould your hands to the cheeks and sides of the jaw and move them slowly apart, upward, and off the sides.

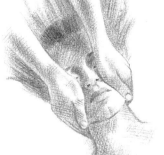

5 Head and scalp

Continue the previous upward movement. Slide your fingers and palms along the sides of the face, over the scalp. Draw your fingers together and come off the top of the head through the hair.

The feet

The human foot is a marvellously complex structure. It is constructed of two arches and twenty-six small bones held together by a dense weave of ligaments, tendons, and muscles. The sole of the foot acts as a shock absorber. It contains a rich concentration of nerve endings and blood vessels, making it highly sensitive to touch. Massaging the feet inevitably restores their spring and agility and improves suppleness. In addition it promotes circulation and reduces fluid retention. Standing or walking a lot places strain on the ankles and feet, so make sure they are both as relaxed as possible–rotate your ankles, flex your feet, and bend them from side to side. For a foot massage, receivers can lie either on their back or their front. Strokes on the feet should be deep and firm.

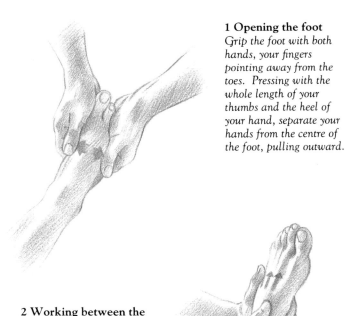

1 Opening the foot
Grip the foot with both hands, your fingers pointing away from the toes. Pressing with the whole length of your thumbs and the heel of your hand, separate your hands from the centre of the foot, pulling outward.

2 Working between the tendons
Hold the sole of the foot with one hand, keeping the toes pointed up. Use the thumb of your other hand to press slowly along the grooves between the tendons that run from the base of the ankle to the toes.

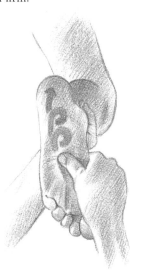

3 Thumbing the sole
Support the foot with one hand. Use your thumb to trace deep rotary movements along the sole. Begin at the ball of the foot and travel toward the heel.

4 Wiggling the toes
On each toe separately, hold the base between your thumb and fingers. Alternately tug and wiggle until your fingers slide off the tip.

5 Stroking the foot
Hold the foot between your hands, your fingers pointing away from the toes. Pull your hands slowly towards you, coming gently off at the toes.

Foot reflexology

Like acupressure (see pp. 165-8), reflexology works by applying pressure to particular points on the skin surface. Each point is related to a particular part of the body, via energy channels or meridians. Deeply relaxing, the treatment consists of deep, steady pressing and rolling movements made using the edge of the thumb. The object is to improve energy, to restore healthy circulation and the elimination of toxins, and to diagnose and relieve pains and minor ailments by stimulating the body's own healing processes. Reflexology is not easy to master–it is best to learn it by going to classes. Most techniques are done with one hand holding the foot steady, the other working the reflexes with thumb or index finger. There may be mild discomfort when you press on some of the reflex points on the side of the foot: do not continue if the process becomes too painful for the receiver.

These foot maps concentrate on the zones and organs most closely linked to stress and stress-related disorders. More detailed maps are also available, and these give a wider variety of reflex points.

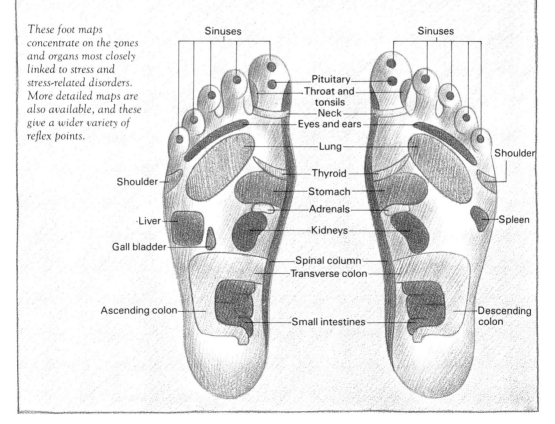

Hands

Tension can build up gradually and imperceptibly in the fingers and wrists. This can be due either to anxiety and worry or to performing tasks that require a great degree of manual dexterity and control. Stiffness in the finger joints can be caused by faulty circulation or arthritis, while chilblains may occur in cold weather as a result of impaired circulation in the hands and feet. Massaging the hands helps in preventing or relieving the discomfort and deformation of arthritis. In addition, it can make you more aware of how and when to relax your hands, relieving tension, encouraging greater mobility, and improving circulation.

1 Opening the palm
Take hold of your partner's hand with the heel of your own hand pressed against the back, your fingers on the palm. Squeeze and stretch the hand open by pulling the fingers away from each other, pressing the heels of your hands down in a counterpull.

2 Working between the bones
Holding your partner's wrist to support the hand, use your thumb and index finger to massage along the channels between the bones of the hand. Work from the wrist to the webs between the fingers.

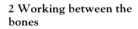

3 Wringing the fingers
Grasp the wrist in one hand as before, and then hold the thumb and other fingers in turn with your other hand. Stretch and twist them as you work your way over both knuckles and off the tips.

Whole-body sequence

How extensive a massage you give depends on the amount of time you have. You may decide to concentrate on particular tension spots, but a whole-body massage is worthwile if you have the time–anything from 45 minutes to an hour and a half. If you are giving an all-over massage, follow a basic sequence of steps. Start by oiling the back. Then, using a variety of strokes, concentrate on specific areas. Graduate from light, broad, expansive strokes, to smaller, deeper, more probing ones. Work on the back of the body, legs, and feet, then on the front, including the face and the hands. If the neck, shoulders, and head are tense and need special attention, end the session with some extra time for these areas.

The back of the body
Begin by using broad expansive strokes that encompass the entire length and breadth of the back. Then focus on individual areas such as the small of the back, the shoulderblades, the upper back, the backs of the shoulders, and the spinal column. You should also massage the buttocks and the backs of the legs.

The front of the body
Ask your partner to turn over and then massage the fronts of the legs, followed by the feet. Massage each arm and hand separately, and then the front of the torso. Here you should concentrate on the sides, the solar plexus, and the ribcage. Next, work your way to the face, moving from the forehead to the chin and from the centre out to the hairline, temples, and ears. Finally, massage the shoulders, neck, and scalp. These are often the areas of greatest tension. End the massage using long, "linking" strokes over the whole body.

Aromatherapy

Essential oils are distilled from a wide variety of fruits, plants, and herbs. Their action on mind and body is subtle and profound. When inhaled, they act on the brain and nervous system via the stimulus of the olfactory nerves, helping to alter mood, dispel fatigue or irritability, and alleviate depression or anxiety. There is also some evidence that they may be partly absorbed through the skin, allowing their more powerful, active constituents to be released into the tissues and the bloodstream. Tests show that oil of lavender rubbed on to the skin of a guinea pig shows up in the urine in less than an hour. You use essential oils in several ways: inhaling them directly from a bottle; using them as a burning essence to pervade the air; adding them to the bath water, allowing their fragrance to be released through the steam; or incorporating them into massage oil for direct application on the face or body. The oils must be stored in a cool, dark place to preserve their therapeutic properties. In order to be effective, the oils must be 100 per cent pure, free of chemical additives and artificial fragrances. Costly to manufacture in the first place, the best essential oils are not cheap, so make sure the oils you use are pure.

Store essential oils in dark, sealed containers. The chart shows which oils are effective for a range of disorders.

AROMATHERAPY	
Problem	**Oils recommended**
Faulty circulation, fluid retention, lethargy, depression	Basil, bergamot, camomile, clary, jasmine, juniper, lavender, melissa, neroli, orange blossom, rose, rosemary, sage, ylang ylang
Nervous tension, sleeplessness, irritability	Clary, cypress, marjoram, rose, sandalwood, sage
Wounds, burns	Benzoin, bergamot, camoline, camphor, eucalyptus, hyssop, juniper
Bruises	Camphor, hyssop, pennyroyal
Catarrh, sinus problems	Cedarwood, eucalyptus, frankincense, hyssop, lavender, myrrh, peppermint
Colds	Basil, black pepper, camphor, eucalyptus, marjoram, peppermint, rosemary

Acupressure

This type of therapy is similar to acupuncture, but you use finger pressure instead of needles. It has been used in the East for centuries to treat aches and pains, overcome tirdeness, and reduce tension. The principle is that finger pressure on specific points on the body stimulates or sedates the flow of vital energy (or ch'i) along channels or meridians. The points and meridians correspond to those illustrated in acupuncture charts.

The intensity of the pressure you should use and the way in which you move the thumb or finger over the point depend on the condition being treated. Nervous tension and stress-related disorders usually require sedation of specific points. You achieve this by exerting pressure on the point and moving your thumb or finger counterclockwise. If stimulating a point (as you would when treating tiredness or lack of energy), apply greater pressure and move your finger clockwise. You can use your thumb, middle finger, or index finger, whichever feels the most comfortable. Keep up the pressure for at least 20 seconds at a time, although prolonged pressure and rubbing the point for a few minutes may be necesary to bring relief. Refer to the pictures shown here to locate the points you wish to treat. You will know that you have found the exact point when the person you are treating feels some tenderness or discomfort.

Pressure techniqes
Acupressure can be used as a self-help technique, but it is more effective if you practise it on someone else. You will be able to exert more pressure, while the receiver will be more relaxed. Cradle the head and body of the receiver (below), so that they feel safe and comfortable, and keep close body contact. Your hands should be relaxed and your mind calm. Breathe slowly and try to exhale as the other person inhales, to achieve a harmonious interchange of energy. If you find a point difficult to locate exactly, try pressing with a narrow, blunt object (below left).

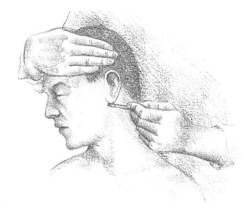

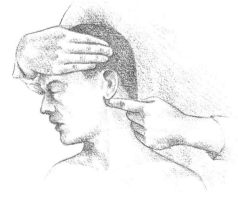

Face and head

Of the many disorders that you can treat with facial acupressure, the following respond particularly well: eye strain, tiredness, headache, sinus congestion, toothache, neuralgia, migraine, catarrh, and general muscular tension. Locate facial points by gently pressing until increased tenderness indicates the point that requires treatment. Press with the pad of your finger–do not damage the skin with your nail. When working around the eyes never press the upper eyelid.

Use the point between the eyebrows to relieve eye disorders and giddiness as well as disorders of the stomach and lower leg. The two points by the inner eye are related to eyestrain and stomach problems. The upper lip point controls sneezing, while treating the chin point can relieve menopausal complaints.

Treating the face points
Cradle the head in one hand. Ask the receiver to relax and let the weight of the head drop completely.

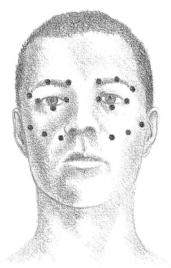

The points along the eyebrows and lower eye sockets affect eystrain, poor concentration, and sinus congestion. They also correspond to the stomach and liver. Press further points along the cheekbone to reduce sinus inflammation and counteract fluid retention in the tissues around the eyes.

Treating the eye points
Pressure along the eyebrows can be firm and prolonged, but be gentler when pressing the lower eyelid.

Use these points for the following disorders.

1 *Sinus problems; hay fever; other allergies.*

2 *Eyestrain.*

3 *Neuralgia and muscular tension.*

4 *Stomach, abdomen, heart, lungs, and eye disorders.*

5 *Disorders of the kidneys, colon, and spinal nerves. Pressure on these points will also relieve headache and tension.*

6 *General relaxation. The head points can also treat pressure headaches and indigestion.*

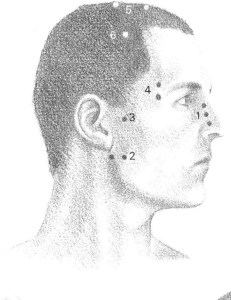

Treating the sinus points
Using a blunt probe such as a rounded pen helps locate small, concentrated points.

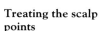

Treating the scalp points
Press gently and slowly with a probe, working over one small section of the scalp at a time.

The series of points along the top of the neck near the hairline can be pressed to treat indigestion, flatulence, headache, nosebleeds, and eye problems.

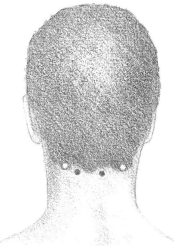

Treating the neck points
Hold the head in the crook of your arm, with the flat of your hand on the crown.

The points on the body

The most easily treated points on the body are on either side of the upper spine at the back of the neck, along the shoulders, at the base of the spine, above the pubic bone, and on the hand. These points may need firm, prolonged pressure in order to obtain lasting relief.

Treating the neck and shoulder points

Treat these together. Use both thumbs to press both sides simultaneously. Headache, migraine, pain, and tension respond well to treatment in this area. Use your thumbs or middle fingers to press on both sides of the spinal column, working downward.

Treating the lower back points

Press the two points on either side of the spine in the lower back to relieve lower back pain, abdominal tension, and pains in the leg and hip. Treatment is easier if the receiver is sitting down, keeping the back straight.

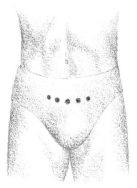

Gentle pressure on points along the top of the pubic bone can alleviate menstrual cramp and pelvic congestion, and counteract sexual and urinary problems.

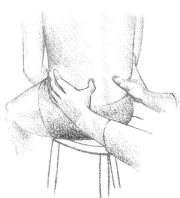

The Hoku point

This point, located in the middle of the fleshy web between the thumb and forefinger is one of the most accessible sedation points for pain relief. Use it to treat migraine, headache, and neuralgia.

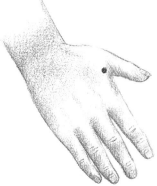

Treating the Hoku point

Pinch the point between the thumb and forefinger and keep up constant pressure for up to five minutes.

HIGH-STRESS
SITUATIONS

Stress solutions

There are problems in even the most stress-free life. Crises occur in weird, often unpredictable ways. The healthiest attitude is to accept life's problems as an inevitable aspect of the normal and diverse challenges of living. But our personal survival skills are not always strong enough to allow us to do this, even if we have a lifestyle that is generally well organized, relaxed, and healthy.

Crises materialize in a multitude of guises and an infinite variety of combinations. The stress of coping with a fretful, ever-wakeful new baby may be accompanied by the strain of post-natal depression. Both could be compounded by any number of major or minor domestic, environmental, or financial irritations. The permutations are infinitely variable, the causes often as unforeseen as the effects. Anticipating the sources of stress in our lives and the problems it is likely to cause is helpful. But in many cases stressful events descend like a bolt out of the blue, catching us unawares. This type of stress is probably the hardest with which to come to grips. No one can predict the major catastrophes such as bereavement, severe illness, divorce, or accidents such as floods, fires or physical assault. Should we fall victim to any of these, our immediate and long-term survival depends on knowing the tactics that will best help us get through the very worst initial shock and trauma.

The charts on the following pages offer a range of solutions to stressful problems, life crises, and stress-related illnesses. Because of their diversity, the problems covered are divided into these categories: general health problems, sexual problems, emotional and behavioural problems, life crises, upheavals, environmental stresses, and work stresses.

There is, of course, rarely a simple or single solution to any problem, no matter how large or small. The situation is made worse, because under stress it is often difficult to remain aware of the choices of action open to us. But if you can remain aware of your options you will be prevented from panicking and taking the wrong decisions in haste, so that you will be able to determine the most expedient course of action. That is why, in trying to suggest the different ways in which you can deal with stressful situations, the chart offers both short-term solutions and long-term strategies. The first category offers as many choices as possible for alleviating the immediate symptoms or effects of the stress factor. The second suggests some strategies you might use in attempting to eliminate the underlying cause. So when trouble or crisis flares up unexpectedly, start by checking the list of short-term solutions for immediate ways you might try to defuse the situation. If the problem is a complex or persistent one, consult the category of possible long-term solutions for ways in which you might come to grips with the fundamental cause or avoid repetition of the crisis. This chapter is extensive but by no means comprehensive. There is unfortunately not enough room to include every health, sexual, domestic, or emotional problem, and every life crisis that might occur. But it does include those most commonly experienced by the majority of individuals and offers many useful tools for your personal survival kit.

General health problems

PROBLEM	SHORT-TERM SOLUTION	LONG-TERM STRATEGY
Migraine	Lie down in a darkened room or wear dark glasses. *Orthodox* Take the usual medication at earliest symptom. Take anti-sickness pills. *Alternative* Have a head and neck massage (pp. 158-9) Press Hoku pain point on hand (p. 168).	Check diet for trigger foods such as chocolate, alcohol (especially red wine), cheese, citrus fruit. Take feverfew herb daily. Learn yoga (pp. 133-45), biofeedback, or autogenics (p. 188). Try a course of acupuncture, or use foot reflexology (p. 161). Check your menstrual cycle to find out whether migraine attacks are linked to ovulation, or the pre-menstrual or menstrual periods. Practice relaxation techniques (p. 102-13).
Headache	Have a good night's sleep. Have something to eat. *Orthodox* As for migraine, but omit migraine medication. Take the painkiller that is most effective for you. *Alternative* Do relaxation exercises for neck, head, and shoulders (pp. 104-7). Put a warm, dry cloth or a cold, wet one (whichever feels better) over face, head, or neck. Massage temples and scalp (pp. 158-9) or try acupressure (pp. 166-7).	Use the relaxation techniques that work best for you (p. 102-13).
Backache	Try a new relaxation position— choose one in which you feel comfortable and do not adopt any position that adds to the pain. Try one of these: lie down, knees on chest; lie down and twist hips and thighs from side to side; hang upside down (p. 112). Move about, stretch your spine, and don't sit in one position for more than 30 mins. If the pain is too great for any of these, lie still on a flat board. Have a hot bath, which will help you to relax. Rub embrocation cream into the affected area or apply heat to it.	Change your mattress or try putting a board under it. Change your chair (p. 89). Keep your back straight when picking up heavy objects. Don't spend long periods standing, bending, or carrying heavy items. Stop for a quiet period of relaxation every two hours. *Orthodox* Have an X-ray. See your doctor if you have any weakness, numbness, or tingling feelings in your legs. *Alternative* Try acupuncture, Alexander technique, Rolfing, osteopathy (pp. 188-9).

PROBLEM	SHORT-TERM SOLUTION	LONG-TERM STRATEGY
Digestion problems	Rest and eat nothing for the first day. On the second day drink diluted, unsweetened fruit juices. On the third day, begin eating foods that you know "agree" with you.	Alter your eating habits. Eat less fat and more fibre (pp. 92-5); eliminate any foods that obviously do not agree with you.
Hay fever	Stay inside when the pollen count is high. Wear dark glasses outside in bright light. *Orthodox* Try anti-histamine tablets, but beware of the drowsiness they can cause. *Alternative* Take homeopathic remedies which have no side effects. Inhale essential oils–eucalyptus, camphor, peppermint (p. 164).	Fit ionizers in main rooms at home and work. Try preventive injections during the winter months. You can develop hay fever as a result of stress, so try relaxation exercises (pp. 102-13) or other relaxation techniques.
Allergy	Go on a rotation diet leaving out main groups of food for three or four days at a time. Test reaction when you reintroduce these into the diet. Stay off foods that aggravate the body's stress response–e.g. sugar, caffeine, salt, (pp. 92-5).	Avoid known contaminants and allergens. Check processed food for suspect additives. Visit a clinical ecologist or allergy specialist for a provocation test and possible desensitizing treatment.
Skin problems	Apply calamine lotion or bland emollient cream.	Check diet for possible allergens. Check clothes, jewellery, make-up, toiletries, watch strap, and bra links for possible irritating chemicals. Try hypnotherapy or biofeedback if the disorder is linked to stress.
Hair loss (women)	Avoid vigorous brushing and combing. Do not pull or tug hair or tie it tightly in a pony tail. Avoid rubber bands, tight clips and combs, perming, bleaching, and dyeing.	Massage the scalp daily to improve circulation. Have a back, shoulder, and head massage (pp. 156-9). Check diet, stress levels. **Note:** Having a baby can cause temporary hair loss; so too can some feverish illnesses and a few drugs.
Sinus problems	Keep your home well ventilated. Use burning essence or scented candles. *Alternative* Inhale eucalyptus oil (p. 164). Try acupressure (pp. 166-7).	Use ionizers. Check your sensitivity to mucus-forming dairy foods. Test for other allergies especially dust, animals, and fibres.

PROBLEM	SHORT-TERM SOLUTION	LONG-TERM STRATEGY
Common cold	Try to remain in an even temperature. Take one gram of Vitamin C every two hours when first symptoms arise. *Alternative* Drink warmed wine and spices, or garlic and onion soup. Try aromatherapy (p. 164).	If persistent, check diet for sufficient intake of fresh fruit and vegetables. Increase your consumption of citrus fruits. Frequent colds may be stress-related, so try regular relaxation exercises (pp. 102-13).
Pre-menstrual tension	Do relaxation exercises (pp. 102-13). Get more sleep. Cut down on social activities. Wear loose clothes. Cut down on fluids. Drink decaffeinated coffee, or camomile tea. *Alternative* Take natural tranquillizers such as Dolomite, Valerian, Passiflora.	Take extra quantities of Vitamin B6, Zinc, and Oil of Evening Primrose about ten days prior to your period. Cut down on caffeine, sugar, and salt at that time. Eat frequent small amounts, avoiding large meals. Ask your physician's advice about going on the pill.
Oedema	Drink freshly pressed vegetable and fruit juices. Drink six to eight glasses of mineral water. *Alternative* Take a herbal diuretic.	Consult your physician about kidney function and general health. Cut down on salt and spices. Stop taking the pill or try a change of brand.
Weight gain	Cut down on all sweet sugary foods, alcohol, sweet drinks, processed foods, and fatty foods. Go on a three- to seven-day cleansing diet consisting of fresh fruit and vegetables, fresh vegetable and fruit juices, and brown rice.	Retrain eating habits and work on a permanent plan for healthy eating. Set your goal—one to two pounds a week weight loss. Start exercising regularly. Ask physician to check thyroid function especially if weight gain is accompanied by tiredness.
Menstrual cramp	Lie or sit with your legs raised. Drink decaffeinated tea or fruit juices. Place a heated pad against the base of your spine. Do gentle exercises. Use sanitary towels rather than tampons. Wear loose clothing. Get plenty of sleep. *Orthodox* Take your usual pain killer.	Try acupuncture, hypnosis, or other relaxation techniques. Pre-plan your social calendar and adjust work schedule. Have a medical check-up for possible fibroids or endometriosis. If you are using an IUD, consider chaging to another method of contraception.
Burns, cuts, accident-proneness	For burns, plunge the affected part immediately into cold water. Apply yoghurt, sour milk, tomato, or vinegar (all acidic). *Orthodox* Use anti-burn cream.	Take extra vitamin E, vitamin C, and zinc and apply vitamin E oil externally to help speed healing and lessen the risk of scarring. Use relaxation techniques (pp. 102-13) to calm you down and help prevent accidents.

Sexual problems

PROBLEM	SHORT-TERM SOLUTION	LONG-TERM STRATEGY
Erection problems	Don't worry about an occasional failure–everyone has them, and anxiety makes the problem worse. Ask your partner to give you the stimulation you like best. Conjure up your favourite sexual fantasy. Don't keep trying if nothing seems to work–settle for a loving cuddle instead.	Have sex only when you are relaxed and in the right mood, and not if you are tired or have been drinking heavily. If the problem starts to happen often, don't even try to have intercourse for a while–enjoy the type of sex play that gives you an erection. When your confidence has built up, try again. If you never have erections– even on waking–consult your physician.
Premature ejaculation	Try again if you can regain your erection. When you are less intensely excited you will probably last longer. Make sure your partner is fully aroused before intercourse begins. Make your own movements less vigorous and stimulating. Try sex with your partner on top.	Learn to recognize the feelings that lead up to orgasm by masturbating. Stop when you feel you are about to come, and stave off the orgasm as long as possible. Then try to do the same during intercourse, pausing each time you are near orgasm.
Inability to reach orgasm (women)	Don't try too hard. Try not to worry about it; discuss the problem with your partner. Conjure up a favourite sexual fantasy. Try new practises, and different positions. Move your body to increase sensation. Make sure you are sexually excited before you begin intercourse. Try exercises (pp. 102-13) before sex if you feel tense.	Work on sexual fantasies. Use books, pictures. Practise pelvic exercises. Try making love in different places and at different times–ensure that you have enough time and privacy. Get to know your body's pleasure zones and best responses. Discuss these with partner. Check fatigue, stress levels. Visit a sex therapist.
Lack of desire	Don't worry about it; discuss it openly with your partner. Use fantasies or sex aids. Be patient. Use masturbation if one partner wants sex and the other doesn't.	Come off the pill or change the brand. Check fatigue and stress levels and make sure that you are getting adequate rest and relaxation. Work on sexual fantasies. Use creative imagery (pp. 152-3). Take a course of Gin seng, B complex vitamins, vitamin E. Look for an underlying problem and try to solve it. Have a holiday. Check hormone levels.

PROBLEM	SHORT-TERM SOLUTION	LONG-TERM STRATEGY
Fear of intercourse	Talk about it with your partner. Try to relax mind and body. Use relaxation exercises (p. 102-13). Get in the mood with the right music, lighting, fragrance, and clothing. Have a couple of glasses of wine. Use KY jelly. Make sure you are sufficiently aroused before intercourse. Experiment with new positions and techniques. Push slightly with your vaginal muscles as your partner enters you.	Learn that penetration need not be painful. The following technique should help you to do this. Using KY jelly, insert one finger, then two, into your vagina. Tighten and then relax the muscles around them. Use tampons so that you become more used to and less fearful about your body.
Difficulty in conceiving	Relax. Try not to worry.	Work out your precise ovulation date (14 days before your period). Have a few days' abstinence beforehand, then make love frequently immediately before, during, after the ovulation date. Visit a specialist for hormone or sperm count tests. Avoid getting too tired or drinking too heavily. Check your reaction to prescribed drugs.
Problems with the pill (mood swings, fluid retention, weight gain, bleeding)	If you have just started taking the pill, give it two to three months' trial. But stop if severe symptoms occur.	Come off the pill or change the brand. Take extra Vitamin B6, zinc, and folic acid.
Problems with the IUD (bleeding, cramp, tension)	Call your physician for on-the-spot advice; this is especially important if bleeding occurs between periods.	Check each month that your IUD is still in place. Have it checked or taken out if problems persist.
Problems with the cap (fiddly, messy, unspontaneous)	Insert in advance. Try adopting a routine: insert the cap regularly every day at the same time after bathing. Always use a spermicide as well. Leave in for six hours after intercourse.	Have regular checks to make sure fitting is correct. Check for damage regularly. Refit at least once a year and after pregnancy.
Problems with the sheath (fiddly, unspontaneous)	Discuss openly and with humour with your partner. Hold the sheath securely during withdrawal. Always use a spermicide as well. Take turns in using your own barrier method so neither of you feels you are getting a raw deal.	If it causes real problems change to another method of contraception.

Emotional and behavioural problems

PROBLEM	SHORT-TERM SOLUTION	LONG-TERM STRATEGY
Panic attacks	During a panic attack, remember that however frightened you feel, it won't hurt you and it will pass. Face the feelings: don't try to fight them as this only intensifies the panic. Use the "stop" relaxation exercise (p.48) or one of the breathing exercises (see pp. 129-31). For night-time panic, get up and do some relaxation exercises (pp. 102-13), or yoga (pp. 133-45), or try making love.	Concentrate as much as you can on the present, to stop yourself worrying about the future. If your anxiety is caused by a particular stress, take what steps you can to remove this. Talk about the experience that has given rise to the anxiety with someone whom you can trust to be understanding. Take regular exercise. Whenever you start to feel tense, use relaxation techniques (pp. 102-13) or breathing exercises (pp. 129-31).
Depression	Acknowledge the emotion and keep in touch with it. Don't be afraid to cry. Make sure you get plenty of sleep. Try to work out what is causing the depression. If desperate, call a close friend, family member, or the Samaritans. Occupy yourself as much as you can. Avoid solitude—see friends and talk it over with them. Try to look at things in a more positive way. Take positive action about a problem if you can. Concentrate on the way things are now—not on the past or future.	Check if the condition is cyclical and coincides with the premenstrual period. Try to eat sensibly. Take up regular vigorous exercise. See a physician if you are so depressed that you cannot eat or sleep properly and seem to have no energy. Visit a counsellor or support group. Avoid making major decisions when depressed. Orthodox medicine can help with depression, but the treatment involves drugs.
Phobias	Avoid the source of the phobia. Try simple exercises for breathing (pp. 129-31) or general relaxation (pp. 112-13). Use the "stop" relaxation technique (pp. 48-9). Try visualization (pp. 152-3).	Try to de-sensitize yourself gradually, looking at pictures of whatever you fear, before facing up to it for a short time, followed by a longer subjection to the source of the phobia. If this fails, seek professional help.
Fatigue	Don't try to fight the fatigue: sleep as long as you can and go to bed early every night. Eat small amounts of complex carbohydrate foods regularly throughout the day.	If caused by stress, accept this as an emotional/depressive state. Take a course of B complex vitamin pills or Gin seng. Have a holiday. Take up gentle exercises. Use creative imagery (pp. 152-3). Cut out mood foods. Check for allergy.

PROBLEM	SHORT-TERM SOLUTION	LONG-TERM STRATEGY
Irritability	Check if pre-menstrual. Take Dolomite, Valerian, or Passiflora. Go out for a long run or a swim. Take an aerobics class (pp. 96-8).	Cut down on coffee, tea, salt, and sugar. Try to stop smoking cigarettes. Use relaxation techniques (pp. 102-13) or autogenics. Take up yoga (pp. 133-45) and meditation (pp. 147-53). Avoid alcohol and do not drive in heavy traffic unless you have to.
Overeating	Throw out all stores of fattening food. Eat fruit, vegetables, or bran before meals to suppress your appetite. You can also try appetite suppressant sweets or chewing gum. Go out for a long run. Put warning signs on fridge door. Put photo of ideal body on bathroom wall. If you are overeating as a result of boredom, make sure you are occupied—go out, meet friends, join clubs or societies and take up new interests or hobbies.	Check emotional state, stress. Adopt a healthy, balanced diet. Take up regular exercise. Join a slimming club or support group. Try acupressure using ear point (p. 167).
Loneliness	Call or visit a close friend. Go to an art gallery, a concert, or to an open-air meeting where there may be an interchange of views amongst participants. Write a letter to someone you care about. Reply to an advertisement in a lonely hearts column. Join an organization that promotes group activities. If you are worried about meeting new people, practice relaxation techniques (pp. 102-13).	Join a club or group that centres on your main interests. Get a flat-mate. Go to evening classes. Form a group with people who have similar problems. Join a gym, tennis club, or health club. Change jobs. Apply for an exchange job with somebody from another country. Get a dog or cat.
Dependence on alcohol	Set yourself reasonable limits (say, two pints of beer or four single whiskies a day). Give yourself two or three alcohol-free days a week. Drink slowly, and always eat when you're drinking. Never drink alone and cut out lunch-time drinking. Don't keep alcoholic drinks at home. Do not meet friends or colleagues in pubs or wine bars. Learn that it is socially acceptable to refuse a drink, whatever others say.	Keep up your short-term measures. If these do not work, phone support group or crisis centre. Try group therapy. Regulate stress level and work load.

PROBLEM	SHORT-TERM SOLUTION	LONG-TERM STRATEGY
Cigarette smoking	Give up completely now. Use nicotine-flavoured chewing gum or herbal cigarettes.	Try relaxation exercises (p. 102-13), acupuncture of the ear, hypnosis, or aversion therapy. Reward yourself by spending the money you save on something you want. Avoid places or activities you associate with smoking. Don't worry if you put on weight at first.
Addiction to tranquillizers	Cut down on the tranquillizers gradually. It is important to do this under the supervision of your physician. This is because you may suffer withdrawal symptoms and depression. Replace the drugs with natural tranquillizers, such as Valerian, Passiflora, or Dolomite.	Try a support group, or alternatives like hypnosis, autogenics, meditation, and acupuncture.
Sleeplessness	If noise is a problem, wear ear plugs to block it out. Take Tryptophan capsules, Dolomite, Calcium, Valerian, or Passiflora. Drink a hot milky drink before bedtime. Eat protein and carbohydrate-rich foods in the evening and avoid tea and coffee, especially at this time. Eat your evening meal earlier. Reduce your alcohol intake. Open a window in your bedroom. If you still cannot sleep, try doing something to help you relax or to use up your surplus energy: make love; get up and do something around the house; do some work; meditate (pp. 147-53); or do relaxation exercises (p. 102-13).	Buy a better bed or mattress. Relax and unwind before bedtime. Take more daily exercise. Go without sleep till you are too tired to stay awake. Take cat naps in the day, sleep less at night. Have massage to relax the muscles.
Inability to relax	Try the "stop" relaxation exercise (p. 48) to calm you down. Do simple relaxation exercises (pp. 102-13). See also the advice under Sleeplessness, above.	Learn one of the relaxation techniques in this book. Amongst the best that you can do by yourself are simple exercises (pp. 102-13), yoga (pp. 133-45), and meditation (pp. 147-53). Autogenics and hypnosis are also very effective, if you want to visit a therapist. If you feel that you need to release a large amount of surplus energy, exercise vigorously every day.

Family problems

PROBLEM	SHORT-TERM SOLUTION	LONG-TERM STRATEGY
Post-natal depression	Get as much sleep and rest as possible. Eat a healthy balanced diet. Take extra B complex vitamins. Ask your partner or relatives to help with child-minding.	Take a holiday. Begin exercising. Employ a nanny and plan to go back to work. If you are so depressed that you can neither enjoy life nor care for your baby, consult your physician.
Menopause	Use clothes and bedclothes made of natural fibres to reduce night sweats. If dryness is a problem use hormone cream or vaseline to assist vaginal lubrication. Avoid caffeine if you are feeling irritable. Make sure that you get plenty of rest and sleep. Reduce your intake of alcohol to counteract hot flushes.	Consult a physician about hormone replacement therapy. Make sure this includes testosterone if low libido is a problem. Change your hairstyle, make-up, or clothes for a new image. Take Dolomite, Calcium, Valerian, to help you sleep.
Divorce	Ensure you have a good and sympathetic lawyer or solicitor. Keep in contact with friends and family. Make sure you recognize and express your feelings–don't try and cover up your feelings or pretend you are coping well when you are not. Keep busy. Get enough sleep and rest. Reduce your intake of alcohol and caffeine. Smoke fewer cigarettes. Try to avoid tranquillizers (see the advice under Bereavement, below).	Divorce is a kind of bereavement, so follow the advice under Bereavement, below. Try to get out and meet friends. Travel. Study a new skill. Change jobs.
Bereavement	Cry. Talk. Acknowledge your feelings and express them if you can. Try to avoid tranquillizers and if you do take them, do so for no more than about one month as they are addictive and will interfere with your ability to express feelings. Don't pretend you are coping well if you are not. Contact an organization for the bereaved if you need help. Contact a lawyer, solicitor, or accountant for further help.	Be prepared to go through a mourning period that may last for as much as two or more years. Recognize that any physical ailments, aches and pains may be related to this period of stress. Start to socialize. Visit a counsellor or therapist. Get enough sleep and rest. Eat a healthy balanced diet. Take extra B complex, zinc, to protect against stress. Meditate (pp. 147-53), and get plenty of exercise.

PROBLEM	SHORT-TERM SOLUTION	LONG-TERM STRATEGY
Wedding	Plan everything carefully. Don't arrange too many social acitivies immediately before the day and leave yourself ample time to make any last-minute arrangements. Get plenty of sleep. Avoid arguments with your partner and family. Don't drink too much alcohol on the day. Around this time avoid foods that cause migraine or allergy. Try to fix the date that does not coincide with pre-menstrual tension or menstruation.	Don't expect perfection from yourself or your partner. Talk, laugh together. Find mutual interests. Discuss your views on children, religion, contraception, money, and other practicalities.
Marital rows	Go away calmly and concentrate on your breathing (pp. 127-31). Think things through in private. Use humour. Get out of the house–go running. Sit it out patiently without sulking. Confine the row to the matter in hand–try not to bring up past grievances. When you are calm, sit down and talk it through quietly. Make love after you've made up–don't resort to sex as a substitute for solving the problem.	Question your own attitudes. Don't automatically blame yourself or your partner. Talk through the point of conflict at calm times, not while you are having a row. Concede points, gain others later. Be more assertive–but not aggressive.
Rows with children	Avoid confrontation wherever possible. When there is a row, say no, quietly but authoritatively. Ask for an apology if child is in wrong. Give an apology if you are in wrong. Explain quietly and clearly. Don't be drawn into a shouting match. Stay in control of the situation.	Avoid the issue if possible. Lay down consistent rules and discipline. Be stricter. Be more assertive–it is a test of who is in control. Try distracting compromise, or negotiation rather than confrontation.
Fractious baby	Do what you can to prevent the baby getting bored–give it something to do, to watch, or to play with, depending on its age.	Give the baby a distraction–something to play with or watch. Give the baby more company. Make sure that the baby is not frightened of new situations–if so, allow more time for the baby to get used to anything new. Check whether there is a feeding problem. If the baby is hungry, feed on demand. If the baby is not eating, consult your paediatrician.

PROBLEM	SHORT-TERM SOLUTION	LONG-TERM STRATEGY
Baby's sleeping problems	Feed the baby on demand. Put a dummy in its mouth. Change its nappy. Sing or rock the baby to sleep. Wrap the baby securely before putting it to sleep and make sure that the baby is warm enough.	Try waking the baby for a final feed immediately before you go to bed. Move the baby out of your room so that you get enough sleep yourself. Make sure the baby's room is warm, dark, and quiet.
Problems with in-laws	Don't lose your temper. Invite other friends to weekends, dinners, and family gatherings. Do something together outside the home. Get in a supply of films or videos. Play Trivial Pursuit. Don't make visits a regular frequent habit. If living in, ensure they have a self contained unit.	Talk over with your partner. Be assertive with partner and inlaws. Try to empathize and gain confidence. Resist role playing or games. Give in sometimes for the sake of harmony.
Unfaithful partner	Talk things over openly. Ask direct questions–provided that you really want to know the answers. Decide on immediate action, then act accordingly. Acknowledge and let out your anger and sadness, if not directly at your partner then at an inanimate object. Leave home for a while and go and stay with friends or family.	Avoid recriminations, guilt, helplessness. Avoid taking tranquillizers, drinking too much alcohol, overeating. Separate or divorce. Find a lover. Wait it out. Most affairs blow over in 6-8 months.

Upheavals

PROBLEM	SHORT-TERM SOLUTION	LONG-TERM STRATEGY
House hunting	Write down all your main requirements before you begin the search for somewhere to live. Give estate agents written details of your requirements. Ring estate agents daily to make sure they are working on your behalf. Be firm about prices. Tell estate agent best times for you to visit properties. If the properties are far away or spread out in different areas, ask the estate agent to provide a car for transport. Send a friend out to view properties for you if you find it difficult to make visits or appointments yourself. Ensure you have a buyer for your existing home before making an offer on another.	Don't leave mortgage application till the last minute. Find a cheap conveyancing solicitor who will work quickly. Do not make any attempt to move or pack until exchange of contracts has taken place. "Chains", delay, and gazumping are frequent hazards.
Moving house	Sort out contents of one cupboard and room at a time. Be systematic. Be ruthless and throw out what you can. Do as much advance preparation as you can to avoid a rush on the day you move. Pack everything yourself if you need to save money. Get packing done professionally if you need to save time and energy. Get plenty of rest and sleep.	Don't try to furnish the new home at once. Allow one full day free for the move itself. Get your friends and family to help you to pack and unpack.
Burglary	Report to police at once. Don't touch anything. Have a strong drink or a cup of tea. Let out your anger and aggression. Cry, shout. Write a list of missing objects. Get friends to help clear up. Call locksmith to change locks on door. Call credit card companies and bank to nullify cards immediately and get new numbers. Call insurance company.	Take extra precautions to secure your home including good quality locks on doors and windows. Leave lights and radio on when going out and use a time-switch for longer periods of absence. Instal bars on ground and garden floor windows and doors. Stop papers, have friends take in your mail and check your place. Have your possessions stamped with a serial number to identify them. Don't leave valuables in the car.

PROBLEM	SHORT-TERM SOLUTION	LONG-TERM STRATEGY
Physical attack	Report to the police. Go to hospital or your physician. Call the rape crisis centre or crisis support group for victims of violent crime. Get a good lawyer if you intend to press charges. Apply for legal aid if paying fees might be a problem. Ask a friend or family member to stay with you if you live alone.	Learn self-defence techniques. Buy a mini-alarm. Avoid walking alone in lonely dark streets, country roads, or late at night in car parks. Be alert at all times in large or underground car parks. Visit a therapist to help you get over the shock of being attacked.
Obscene phone calls	Hang up. Challenge the caller using contempt and humour. If they happen often, call the telephone company and ask them to monitor calls. Change your telephone number. If you are female get a man to answer. Make sure you don't leave your name as well as telephone number on your answering machine as they may be able to get your address through the telephone directory. If you are female put a man's voice on the answering machine. Apply for an ex-directory number.	Don't panic. There is nothing that can be done to prevent most obscene phone calls, but callers usually do not know the identity or the address of the person that they are calling. If the problem continues, change your telephone number or apply for an ex-directory number.
Redundancy	Apply for social security. Apply to job centre. Go to temporary employment agency. Call friends or colleagues to find out about work. Buy newspapers and check jobs available. Listen to local radio announcements for jobs available.	Extend your existing skills. Learn new skills. Study for a new career under a government training scheme. Start your own business from home. Start a jobless support group. Plan a routine for each day. Stay active. Don't get up late. Consider moving to another area where the likelihood of getting another job is greater.

Environmental problems

PROBLEM	SHORT-TERM SOLUTION	LONG-TERM STRATEGY
Noise	Wear earplugs at night or during work if possible. Report noise at work to management. Report street noises and incessant night alarms to council or police. Complain to neighbours politely in writing. If this fails, complain face to face. If your neighbours are tenants indicate that you will report them to the landlord. If your neighbours are your own tenants indicate that you may be forced to evict them. Fit carpets in your home, and make children and the rest of family turn down the volume on TV, radio, or stereo. You can use a portable stereo player to cut out slight external noise, but beware of turning up the volume too high–loud music can be just as damaging to your health as other noise.	Relaxation and meditation (pp. 147-53) and a positive attitude can all help to lower irritation and anger when noise reaches an unacceptably high level.
Smell	Trace source and remove. Ventilate rooms frequently. Use scented candles, burn essential oils or scented spray. Grow fragrant plants such as hyacinths. Empty used ash trays regularly. Empty garbage and animal trays daily. Keep dirty linen in a closed container. Hang sachets of dried herbs in clothes cupboards. Wrap pungent-smelling foods in cling film or tin foil. Use air-tight containers. Ask visitors not to smoke; or have a smoker's room. Use an effective deodorant; bathe regularly.	Buy an air ionizer. Use extractor fans in kitchen and bathroom.
Bad lighting	Put on lightly tinted spectacles. Turn off the offending light. Focus working light on a table top, not in your eyes.	Put a dimmer switch on your lights. Fit weaker or tinted bulbs or use full-spectrum lights. Go out of doors without sunglasses in bright weather. Sit by an open window.

PROBLEM	SHORT-TERM SOLUTION	LONG-TERM STRATEGY
Rush-hour	If possible, cycle or walk rather than driving or using public transport. On buses and trains, read, smile, and relax as much as you can. If you have to drive, don't rush. Drive with courtesy to others, leaving plenty of space between your car and the one in front. Use the time to think and relax, and enjoy your "personal space". If there are children in the car, encourage them to look at what is going on outside, not to distract you by getting excited. If the traffic is crawling, use the handbrake and neutral more, to rest your feet. Don't crouch forward at the wheel. Keep the windows closed to exclude noise and listen to relaxing music on the radio. If you are angered, worried, or frustrated by the road conditions, stop, get out of the car, and relax before continuing. Try breathing exercises (pp. 129-31) or the "stop" exercise (p. 48), or acupressure (pp. 166-7).	Try to adjust your schedule to miss the rush-hour. Get in the first or last carriage in the subway. Use the non-smoking sections in trains and buses. Walk along uncrowded back routes even if it takes longer. Take an early or late lunch break when snack bars and restaurants are less crowded. Do shopping early in the morning or on weekdays rather than weekends. Try to take your holidays in the spring or autumn. July and August are the most crowded months in popular holiday resorts, airports and all other modes of transport tend to be very crowded. Allow youself plenty of time to get to work in the mornings in order to avoid panic and anxiety about being late. Fuming and fretting will do nothing to get you there sooner and can only damage your health.
Jet lag	Avoid drinking alcohol during and after the flight. Counteract dehydration by drinking regular amounts of water, fruit juice, or herb teas during and after the flight. Avoid tea and coffee as these have a diuretic effect. Wear loose comfortable clothes. On board, try to lie flat and sleep, and ask not to be disturbed. If sitting up, get up every hour and do stretching, flexing exercises. On arrival, try to go to bed and eat at the right time locally. Eat carbohydrate-rich food and protein to help you sleep. Do yoga, relaxation, or meditation to slip more easily into the new time-zone.	Change the time you go to bed by one hour back or forward each night for a few nights prior to departure. By the time you reach your destination your body rhythm should be more attuned to the new time zone. If travelling to a destination at least five time zones away, follow a four day alternate feast/fast regimen to preset your biological "clock" to new time zone. Day 1: Eat only high protein, high carbohydrate meals; drink caffeine only between 3-5 pm. Day 2: Try to fast as much as possible; eat light, protein foods; caffeine only between 3-5 pm. Day 3: Feast as day 1. Day 4: Fast as day 2. Break the fast at breakfast time in the city of destination regardless of the hour either on plane or at home.

Problems at work

PROBLEM	SHORT-TERM SOLUTION	LONG-TERM STRATEGY
Demotion	Accept at once or complain. Discuss the reasons clearly with your superior.	Look for another job or make the best of your new position: try to excel and get repromotion.
Personality clash at work	Avoid confrontations wherever possible. Be assertive but not hostile. Report the problem to the next superior along. Write a formal complaint, setting out the problems. Make an appointment to see the person concerned and state clearly and politely what the problem is as you see it—be prepared to listen to the other person's point of view but also state your own case clearly and forthrightly.	Leave your job. Try to get the other person placed in another department. If the problem is truly serious and others back you up on your decision try to get the person to leave.
Overwork	Say "no" sometimes. Do not take on too many responsibilities or push yourself too far. Delegate, or ask your superior for extra help if there is no one to delegate to. Manage your time more efficiently and concentrate on one job at a time. Take five-minute breaks every hour and twenty-minute breaks every three hours. Try to do work that requires maximum concentration during the peak of your individual energy curve.	Reassess and redefine your goals and expectations. Change jobs. Try to get help—an assistant or a secretary. Restructure your own way of working. Get enough sleep, leisure time, relaxation. Set firm limits—times and places at which you never work and no-one connected with work may contact you. Put work out of your mind at these times. Eat a healthy diet.
Interview	Have at least ten minutes consciously relaxing before the appointment. Concentrate on breathing and de-tensing jaw, neck, and shoulder muscles. Use positive visualization techniques. Wear smart clean pressed clothes—but do not dress up in anything unusual. Adjust hair and make-up—but do not wear anything new or garish. Visit the lavatory before going in to your appointment.	Study autogenic training, practise meditation (pp. 147-53) and other relaxation techniques, and try creative imagery (p. 152-3) to cope with nerves. Work on personal assertiveness.

Glossary of therapies and techniques

This glossary gives brief details of a number of complementary therapies and exercise and body re-integration techniques that are particularly useful for people under stress and suffering from stress-related illnesses. Most of these require you to consult a qualified therapist or visit a specialist teacher.

Acupuncture

An oriental system of medicine based on the principle that vital energy flows through a network of meridians in the body. Illness is seen as a state of energy imbalance in particular areas – an excess in some parts, a deficiency in others – and needles are inserted at specific points on the body to stimulate or sedate the flow of energy. The technique of acupressure uses finger pressure on the acupuncture points to achieve similar results (see pp. 165–8).

Alexander technique

A system of mind–body re-education which fosters a new way of looking at and "using" the self. Alexander teachers work with pupils on a one-to-one basis, showing them how to inhibit harmful tensions and directing them towards more natural patterns of mind and body use.

Autogenics

A method of mind-over-body control based on a specific discipline for relaxing parts of the body by means of auto-suggestion. Autogenics is learned over a period of weeks and, once learned, the exercises take only a few minutes each day. The appeal of autogenics lies in the depth of the overall relaxation it is possible to achieve.

Biofeedback

A method of measuring, and helping you to control, your level of relaxation. Biofeedback monitoring equipment measures very accurately the changes in finger temperature, skin resistance, brainwave patterns, and blood pressure, which indicate how tense or relaxed you are. Biofeedback training involves using the information provided by the monitoring equipment to help you voluntarily change your responses and thus to promote relaxation.

Chiropractic

A manipulative therapy that aims to correct musculoskeletal disorders and related problems. The treatment techniques used by chiropractors tend to be similar to those of osteopathy. As well as joint problems, other stress-related illnesses, such as headaches, migraine, asthma, and digestive disorders also respond to this type of treatment in some cases.

Dance therapy

The use of dance and movement to promote fitness, good posture, and emotional well-being. Some therapists emphasize the benefits of co-ordination and posture, others encourage elements of free improvization that lead to the breaking down of inhibitions and the venting of underlying emotions.

Feldenkrais technique

A method of body retraining designed to improve posture and overall well-being. The technique aims to help you to recognize and correct bad habits of body use. This is done in two stages. Awareness through movement comprises a course of simple exercises that can be taught to a large group; it may be followed up with functional integration, in which the teacher works one-to-one with the trainee.

Gravity guidance

A technique for easing away the body's stresses and strains and improving posture. It works on the premise that many of the body's strains are caused by the downward pull of gravity, which distorts posture. We should therefore use this force to reverse the negative strains. The main way of doing this is by simply hanging upside-down. This has an effect similar to that of orthopaedic traction and can be helpful for spine and neck problems.

Homeopathy

A system of medicine based on the principle that "like cures like". Homeopaths see the symptoms of a disease as part of the body's way of defending itself from that disease. So homeopathic remedies, if taken in a material dose by a healthy person, would bring on symptoms of the relevant illness; if taken by someone who is ill, they will stimulate the person's vitality to combat the disorder. The other guiding premise of homeopathy is that the process of dilution and succussion (or shaking) a remedy makes it more rather than less potent.

Hydrotherapy

The therapeutic use of water, either taken internally or used externally, including the use of hot and cold baths, Turkish baths, and saunas. The relaxation induced by warm baths and the invigorating effects of saunas are well known and can be useful both in reducing symptoms like back pain, and in removing the causes of stress-related illnesses by helping you to relax.

Hypnotherapy

The use of hypnosis for therapeutic ends. While you are in the hypnotic state, the therapist makes suggestions which influence your subconscious mind. Hypnotherapy is effective in helping people achieve goals that they want to reach but feel unable to, such as giving up smoking.

Naturopathy

A group of related natural-health disciplines used to promote health and to show people how they can alter their lifestyles so as to avoid future illness. The systems involved include hydrotherapy, diet therapy, and relaxation techniques. Naturopathy is concerned with maintaining emotional and physical balances, and looking after the internal environment of the body.

Osteopathy

A system of medicine concerned with the body's structural and mechanical disorders. Osteopathy concentrates on the bones, muscles, and other supportive tissues – the body's framework. By using gentle manipulation it helps the whole body to function correctly.

Index

Index continued

Acknowledgments

Author's acknowledgments

I would like to thank the following people for their help with particular areas of this book:

Geoffrey Blundell (biofeedback and meditation); Dr John Bonn and Beverley Timmins (panic and anxiety states); Malcolm Carruthers (relaxation techniques, the chemistry of stress); Lisa Curtis and Dr Raymond Abrezol (sophrology and guided visualization); Janet Grant and Nancy Paul (assertiveness); Dr Stephen Gullo (relationships); Bernard Hall (exercise); Sandy Hemingway (massage and acupressure); Dr Claud Lum and Dr Christopher Bass (hyperventilation); Dr Peter Nixon (causes and effects of stress); Celia Wright and Barbara Cadwell (nutrition).

Publisher's acknowledgments

Gaia would like to extend thanks to the following:

Sharon Bannister, Dermot Browne, Christene Burgess, Fausto Dorelli, Elizabeth Fenwick, Geraldine, Lesley Gilbert, Chris Gregory, Bernard Hall, Sandy Hemingway, Barbara Karban, Anna Kruger, Caterina Lamanna, Lucy Lidell, Louiza Livingstone, Lucy Oliver, Mary Oliver, John Pattison, Edward Pinner, Martin Rhodes-Schofield, Dr Paul Rosch, Peter Sullivan, Sara Thomas, Marvin Thrush, Danuta Trebos, Michael van Straten, Peter Warren, Nina White, H L Zeech.

Photographic credits

All photographs in this book were taken by Fausto Dorelli, with the following exceptions:

p. 11   Eric Hosking/David Hosking
p. 170   Barnaby's Picture Library

Typesetting

Filmset in Goudy by Filmtype Services Limited, Scarborough, North Yorkshire.

Colour reproduction

Technographic Design and Print Ltd.